CALLING OUT FROM THE PAST

The First Odd Fellows Home in California

Peter V. Sellars

DEDICATION

Dedicated to the memory of Adrian Guilford
My high school history teacher

CONTENTS

ACKNOWLEDGMENTS

This project could not have been as thoroughly completed without the kind assistance of the following people: Lucy C. Sperlin of the Butte County Historical Society for keeping the archives office opened during the Thanksgiving Day weekend; Jane Hernandez for her editing and clarification; Jeremy Ritter for his mastery of digital imaging; my wife Bonnie for her assistance with the research of material; Ron Olson of Oroville Lodge No. 59; the Butte County Historical Society; the Meriam Library at Cal-State University-Chico; the staff at the Oroville Library; the California Historical Society, especially Debra Kaufman and Mary Morganti; and the Butte County Pioneer Museum.

INTRODUCTION

There are many places we call ghost towns. There are places we call historic. Then, there are places that have been forgotten—places of which we have little or no knowledge. Sometimes those places call out to us. One of those places was once a home for the aged, as it was often referred to a century ago. This place was a community that had been established from the desires of a few members into something real.

The Independent Order of Odd Fellows (a prominent organization that came to America in the early 1800s) sought the creation of a home to facilitate its aging members. Through perseverance and an unwavering determination, this so-called home was founded in a place in northern California called Thermalito.

For years, the Odd Fellows in California contemplated the idea of creating a home for its aging members. The organization was already providing a pseudo-type of medical insurance for its ill or physically distressed members, meaning there were financial benefits for those members needing assistance. Other states had these types of homes. This was at a time when the Order—as it was called—was a beneficial society assisting members in sickness and providing a death benefit.

If the Thermalito property had not been enticingly available to the Odd Fellows at a time when it was aggressively seeking land for such an endeavor, it most likely would have never selected such a location. On the onset, the distance from San Francisco and the summer heat of the land site were unpopular with the membership. Still, having a structure, land, an opportunity to expand its new enterprise, and a new value or principle in caring for its older members was overwhelmingly attractive. It was an opportunity to have a starting point, which would be both realistic and educational.

The Odd Fellows, already a very strong and beneficial society in California (even vastly outnumbering the Masons in the 1800s), felt the need to keep up with sister Odd Fellows lodges of other states. Many of the other states had homes for the aged and infirmed. By 1886, the general membership demanded the Grand Lodge build a facility to house those loyal and longtime members, rather than allowing them to fade away and perish in some indignant manner.

Who would have thought that about the same time the Odd Fellows were investigating the creation of a home for its older members, that a private company would be building a hotel in a new "beautiful colony" called Thermalito? And, this project would be a flop? Blame it on the summer heat. Blame it on the poor promotion of sales. This so-called largest hotel in California, north of Sacramento, would conveniently fall in the lap of the Independent Order of Odd Fellows. Timing was everything!

The Odd Fellows did indeed receive a place to house and care for its older and needy members from the generosity of those who failed in promoting a development project. A gift was a gift, saving the Order the question of immediate funding and from those members who were ready to debate the prospect of a home due to the lack of available funds.

No doubt finding the money for such a project would have been the stopping point concerning any kind of residence for these older members. There was an established fund already started a few years earlier for this future dream, but that account certainly did not have the kind of money needed for a care facility. Even the Sovereign Grand Lodge of the I.O.O.F. (the Independent Order of Odd Fellows), that oversaw the entire jurisdiction of the United States, would not permit the Grand Lodge in California to assess subordinate lodges for the purpose of erecting a new home for the aged. If the Odd Fellows were going to have a home, it needed an outside private company to fail. Then, it needed a miracle for that company to say, "Here: this is for you, Odd Fellows." That is almost the way it happened!

Of course, those same reasons and miseries that one group failed and caused the Odd Fellows to gain a new home for its indigent and aged members would be the same arguing point for those individuals who never really accepted Thermalito as the prime location for their home. From the onset, the property in Thermalito would never be seen as a permanent place to house its longtime members. Regardless, if, and when the location of this new home would ever change, hundreds of Odd Fellows would end their days on the property in Thermalito. Hundreds would remain and not ever leave the grounds.

The lessons learned at Thermalito educated an organization insofar that one of the most well devised land expeditions to ever take place was accomplished. Seventeen years after moving into Thermalito, the Odd Fellows located the most perfect properties in Santa Clara County (in what would become a town named Saratoga). Location was the direct result of the lessons learned at Thermalito. Location and proximity to San Francisco (the Odd Fellows headquarters) was first and foremost. The weather, the wells, the soil, the transportation, the surrounding populations, and any other expectations and requirements were met by finding Saint Clara. The memory of Thermalito faded into oblivion.

CHAPTER 1

THE INDEPENDENT ORDER OF ODD FELLOWS

Defining the Independent Order of Odd Fellows is not an easy task. The reason the Odd Fellows is not easily defined is the organization really is not the fraternity it was 200 years ago or even 100 years ago as it has gone through a metamorphosis.

Where its membership in California reached nearly 60,000 in 1927, it now stands at roughly 5,000 in 2008. At one time, nearly one in seven people in California were members of the Odd Fellows. This organization has definitely changed.

On April 26, 1819, Odd Fellows officially came into existence in America when Washington Lodge No. 1 in Baltimore, Maryland, was established. It had originated in England many years earlier. Thomas Wildey, the first Grand Master, was seen as the founder of American Odd Fellowship. He was the Grand Master in Maryland for 12 years.

In short, the Order, as it is also referred to, spread throughout the eastern states and eventually westward, reaching California by 1849. Of course, the Gold Rush helped bring the populace to California, rapidly expanding Odd Fellowship in the state.

The Odd Fellows live by principles, which are taught through various levels of degrees. These principles include: friendship, love, truth, faith, hope, charity, and universal justice. Members promise to uphold certain practices by taking an oath. They promise to visit the sick, relieve the distressed, bury the dead, and educate the orphan.

The name "Odd Fellows" derived from any one or a combination of the following. In the 1700s, it was seen as being uncommon, or "odd," for a group of men to help one another, to come to each other's aid, and to offer social relief. Another source says that during the Roman times,

1

the term "Odd Citizens" was used and then Caesar Titus called these people "Odd Fellows." In the mid-1700s, nontraditional professional workers who did not belong to working unions or guilds were called "odd" and did "odd jobs"; then, when the group officially formed, it took the name of "Odd Fellows" (the latter makes the most sense).

Historically, living up to the principles and performing these good works meant something much more 100 years ago. There were few hospitals, so this meant visiting those in a home or a distant place; and travel was not done by automobile in the 1800s. Relieving the distressed meant sometimes giving a hand to a fellow member; it meant sacrifice of one's time and energy. Years ago, in many cases, burying the dead was seen as an act of honor. For an organization to commit to burying its dead was a great endeavor. Think about this in today's terms. "Educating the orphans"—that statement in itself is enormous and still accomplished by the Order in California. The Order has changed; but the working toward the aforementioned goals through honorable principles deserves recognition and admiration.

The Independent Order of Odd Fellows embraced the idea of creating homes for its elderly and poor members in the 1800s. The idea was well matched with the already-established precepts. California worked very hard to establish a home. It was never perfect, but it was better than the alternative—not having a home.

The Grand Lodge of the United States (later to be renamed the Sovereign Grand Lodge) oversaw all of the Grand Lodges of each state. The Grand Lodge regulated the activities of the subordinate Odd Fellows Lodges and Rebekah Lodges. The Odd Fellows helped establish the first hospital in California, some of the first libraries, and much more. The organization had some of the most prominent members of each city in its lodges. Many of these members joined when the Order first was established in the state in 1849 and in the following years. By the 1880s, these members were reaching old age. Many lacked the means to support themselves because they could no longer labor for survival. Where would they go? How were their last days going to be spent? Some had no families to bear the burden.

Odd Fellowship defined its society as meeting the needs of others. A home was bound to be established.

CHAPTER 2

THE EARLY HOMES

The Odd Fellows prided itself on the precept, "to visit the sick, relieve the distressed, bury the dead, and educate the orphan." But there was probably an overwhelming desire to include the care of elderly and indigent members. Eventually this would evolve into caring for the wives, widows, and orphaned children of these members, and eventually for the Rebekahs—the sister faction of the all-men lodges of early Odd fellowship.

Taking the lead role on establishing a home was Pennsylvania. In April of 1872, the Odd Fellows established a home for the orphaned children at Meadville, Pennsylvania. This was the "first Home created

Odd Fellows Home, Meadville, Pa.

One of the first Odd Fellows homes in the country was established in Meadville, Pennsylvania.

Odd Fellows home in Meadville, Pennsylvania. Meadville was the site of the first Odd Fellows home in the country, which was established in 1872.

by any fraternal society." Later, this was expanded to include elderly members of the Order.

Shortly thereafter, other Odd Fellows in the other cities followed the role of Meadville, Pennsylvania. In 1880, Pittsburg built its Home for Widows and Orphans. Then other states followed: Portland, Oregon, in 1883; New Hampshire in 1883; New Jersey in 1885; Unionport, New York, in 1886; Corsicana, Texas, in 1886; Green Bay, Wisconsin, in 1890; Hollis, New York, in 1891; Massachusetts in 1892; Lockport, New York, in 1893; and yet another in Philadelphia, Pennsylvania, in 1894.

The names of these Odd Fellows homes varied. By today's standards, some of these names could be considered offensive or politically incorrect. There were the Old People's Homes, the Old Folks' Homes, Homes for the Decrepit, and Homes for the Orphans. Now, the few homes the Odd Fellows still maintain are referred to as the "Odd Fellows Homes," or simply, "Retirement Homes."

After the first home was established in Pennsylvania in 1872, the Order across the country felt a new obligation to advance and expand

In 1890, the Odd Fellows in Wisconsin established its home in Green Bay.

Massachusetts established its first Odd Fellows home in 1892.

The Odd Fellows home in Connecticut.

in its precepts, as mentioned above. This is evident as other states did, in fact, build homes, and other states sought homes. This included California. Starting in 1849, Odd Fellowship was relatively new in California. It was still growing. But it had the desire to grow and go beyond the jurisdictions that had a head start.

Without a home for its aged and tired members, California Odd Fellows definitely felt the pressure of establishing a home. By the 1880s, it had established a fund for the "aged" members. In 1886, the Grand Lodge of California appointed "The Special Committee On Odd Fellows Home." Its duty was to "consider the subject of the establishment of an Odd Fellow's Home." This committee was obviously appointed because many in the memberships of the Odd Fellows were pushing the idea of having a place for the older and infirm members.

In 1888, during the Annual Grand Lodge Sessions held at San Francisco, California, "The Special Committee On Odd Fellow's Home" used the Fourteenth Annual Report of the Odd Fellow's Home of the Jurisdiction of Pennsylvania to make its argument for having a home in California. The report on the home in Pennsylvania was extremely favorable. (By this time, Pennsylvania Odd Fellows already had four homes.) Note: Annual reports were normally presented in May of each year.

"The Special Committee on Odd Fellow's Home" also appeared to walk the fence, most likely giving in to some of the membership not ready to accept expanding the roles of Odd Fellowship and take on more costly responsibilities. A home would cost money! The committee did back off on the urgency of needing a home by stating in its report, "let us first provide the foundation, and then build with sound judgment as our requirements dictate." The committee then proceeded to request "further time in which to procure positive offers of prices for suitable plots of lands in several localities of the state." This report would not come before the Grand Lodge Body until the following year. California felt the pressure of establishing a home, yet it was being careful not to disturb the naysayer of the Order.

Members had a right to be concerned and somewhat hesitant about starting a home in California. Things were going well. The Order was continuing to grow. In 1886, there were 24,375 members in California. The Order paid sick benefits to those who qualified. Sick members were being visited. Members who died were being buried. Lodges were coming to the aid of members who were needy. The precepts and values were being met and followed respectively. Adding a home would be taking on a new task. It would mean change.

In 1886, the Sovereign Grand Lodge did not help the placement or the funding of a home. It presented the following resolution: "That State Grand Lodges and Encampments may provide by Constitutional enactment for the erection and maintenance of Homes for the aged and indigent Odd Fellow; provided, however, said Bodies shall not make assessments on Subordinates for the purpose of erecting and maintaining the same." This meant the Grand Lodge of California could not impose any additional dues or per capita on subordinate lodges and apply such funds toward a home. From where was the funding supposed to originate? From the individual members? This meant a majority of the membership would have to truly believe that providing a home was in the best interest of the Order.

CHAPTER 3

SLOW PROGRESSION

If the debate of creating a home for its aged and indigent members was hot in the 1880s, the Odd Fellows in California were now out and out demanding a home in the early 1890s. On May 10, 1892, in San Francisco, during the fortieth Annual Session of the Grand Lodge of California, representative Frederick J. Moll, Sr., of Orpheus Lodge #237 in Los Angeles, stood before the membership and presented a resolution that, in essence, demanded that the Grand Lodge of California provide either a home "for every Odd Fellow who has become old and infirm" or "establish an Odd Fellow's Pension Fund, from which fund aged and infirm Odd Fellows may be sufficiently pensioned to sustain themselves for the balance of their old days." In other words, this resolution was made to force the Grand Lodge to respond. It surely could not afford the creation of a pension fund, but set the urgency in motion for providing a home for its older members. Mr. Moll had the courage to be the member to force the issue. The idea or debate of instituting a home had been going around for the past six years.

The response to Moll's resolution, which had been referred to the State of the Order Committee for recommendation, was somewhat pacifying in that the committee stated, "that the creation of a Pension Fund is neither necessary nor expedient." It further stated, "that as to the matter of an Odd Fellow's Home, we believe there is a constantly increasing demand for such an institution in our Order in this State." Then, the committee suggested Moll's resolution be given to a Special Committee of five, to be appointed by the Grand Master. This Special Committee was to make a report at the next session—in one year.

In 1893, the Special Committee on the Home probably provided one of the most constructive reports since the idea of having a home first arose. It gave a detailed report, which included several ideas and plans for funding a home project. It answered the most important part—which was how to find funding for a new home project. The committee offered a resolution that would have the Grand Lodge elect five trustees to constitute a Board of Management "having full power to regulate its affairs, to make necessary rules for the Home. . ." This was really the establishment of the home's infrastructure before actually having a home. Now a location was needed. This would later prove to be the most debated subject concerning the home.

William H. Barnes was one of the first trustees of the home. He was one of the most beloved members of the Odd Fellows in California.

S. B. Smith served as a trustee on the first home board. He was the home board's third president.

The five trustees who were elected: Charles N. Fox, William H. Barnes, Samuel B. Smith, R. H. Lloyd, and Wesley F. Norcross.

Wesley F. Norcross had been a trustee of the home.

CHAPTER 4

SETTLING ON A LOCATION

The first report of the Trustees of the Odd Fellow's Home was on May 8, 1894. Financing the home was at the core of the report. However, other questions needed answering. Would the home be made available to only members of Odd Fellows Lodges? Would widows and orphans be cared for at this home? How many inmates, as they were called, would be permitted to reside at the home? The trustees had sent questionnaires to all of the subordinate lodges in the state. Many lodges did not respond, which led the trustees to believe there was little interest in having a home, or the membership thought financing of the home should come from an additional source other "than that of mere voluntary contributions."

Concerning the property, 20 acres of land near the city of Stockton was offered as a gift by member R. Gnekow. This was the first plausible offer. However, the trustees reported this land was unimproved and would require much money to prepare it for a home.

There were also various hotels for sale that seemed desirable to the board, and these were included in its report. A 75-room hotel, "fully furnished, ready for immediate occupancy," was available in East San Gabriel for a price of $40,000. There was a 38-room hotel with 2½ acres of land in North Ontario for $12,000. For $10,000, a 40-room hotel with 15 acres in Anaheim could be purchased. And in Mound City, which was between San Bernardino and Redlands, there was "a well-built hotel with sixty rooms surrounded by orange groves on twenty-three acres for $10,000, with the option to purchase more available property." The property had naturally occurring water, which originated from the Bear Valley System.

Trustee Charles Fox spoke highly of the Mound City property. The report quoted Fox as saying the place was "so excellent a site, one so well adapted to the uses desired, and could be secured and made available." The trustees presented some very tempting properties to the Grand Lodge, of which any one choice would have been a good choice. The work by this board was bearing serious fruit. The trustees also included in the report a great concern of the funding once a property was secured. There had been no real long-range planning regarding this issue. Perhaps any one of the mentioned properties could have been obtained, but how would it be supported? Up until this time, not enough money had been committed by the subordinate lodges or individual members to sustain a major operation of operating a home. Even the Grand Lodge only had $1,095.25 in its College and Home Fund. A home would have to wait, unless a miracle happened.

In 1893 and 1894, the trustees for the home had sent questionnaires to all of the Odd Fellows and Rebekah Lodges in the jurisdiction of California. The lodges were asked to provide the number of how many members each would have whom they thought would be eligible to enter a home, once one was established. The lodges were also asked to describe the condition of these members thought to be eligible for a home. It was determined that "about fifty persons" were immediately eligible.

According to the trustees' report submitted in 1895, by September of 1894, "some dozen or fifteen properties had been offered to us as sites for the Home." Up to this point, only the Stockton property was offered as a no-cost gift. Most of the other offers were very good also. However, there was some concern by trustees that all of these other properties were located in Southern California. As a result, in November of 1894, the trustees began to examine new properties in Northern California, first looking in Santa Clara County, about 60 miles south of San Francisco. The price of the property in Santa Clara made the consideration prohibitive. It was also determined by the trustees, that "the climate, though excellent for persons in the vigor of life, was not well adapted to persons suffering from the infirmities of age as any of those examined in the south." That the trustees thought the "climate" of Santa Clara was not well suited is significant in that less than 17 years later, Santa Clara County would end up being the home of the Odd Fellows for the next 100 years! The trustees continued their search in Alameda County, closer to San Francisco; its climate was not desirable either. Matters were soon to change as luck would intervene.

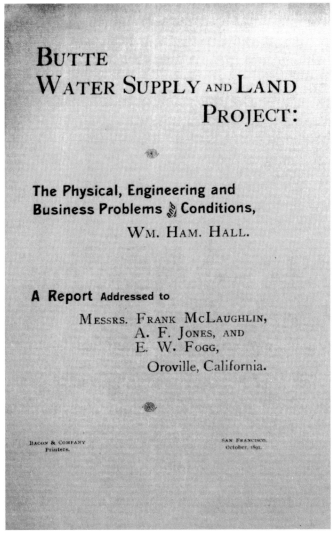

BUTTE
WATER SUPPLY AND LAND
PROJECT:

The Physical, Engineering and
Business Problems & Conditions,

WM. HAM. HALL.

A Report Addressed to
MESSRS. FRANK McLAUGHLIN,
A. F. JONES, AND
E. W. FOGG,
Oroville, California.

BACON & COMPANY
Printers.

SAN FRANCISCO.
October, 1891.

The three donors of the home had the land in the Thermalito area surveyed in 1891.

A member of Oroville Lodge No. 59, Albert F. Jones, who also practiced law in Oroville, approached the trustees to make an offer. As president of the Thermalito Colony Company, Jones was also in a position to not only know what the Odd Fellows needed, but to get the organization what it wanted. He, along with fellow members Major Frank McLaughlin and Mr. Edward W. Fogg, owned the Thermalito Colony Company, and all three generously offered a home to the Odd Fellows.

THERMALITO!

MARVELOUS PROGRESS

OF THE

BEAUTIFUL COLONY

OF

CENTRAL -:- CALIFORNIA

IN ONE YEAR

300 ACRES OF ORANGE GROVES.   12 MILES OF GRADED AVENUES.   9 MILES OF WATER MAINS.

Bella Vista

Hotel,

Largest Hotel in California North of Sacramento.

3,500,000 GALLONS, HOURLY FLOW, OF WATER.

LAND $50 TO $150 PER ACRE--FREE WATER FOR THREE YEARS.

Terms, one-third cash, one-third in one year, one-third in two years, with interest at seven per cent. per annum.

We challenge comparison for beauty of location, mount of improvement, capacity of soil for production, and water powr and supply

Thermalito Colony Company,

Oroville, Butte County, Cailf

MIDDLETON & SHARON, 22 Montgomery St., San Francisco.

34

An 1889 advertisement for the Bella Vista Hotel. The hotel never was in operation.

On November 24, 1894, a new hotel and its surrounding lands in Thermalito were visited by the trustees. This property was the last offered to the Odd Fellows. The properties in and around Thermalito were nothing but vast areas of orange groves. This was considered the "citrus belt of the State." In the middle of this sea of oranges was the Bella Vista Hotel. The hotel was situated on 8 acres of land on the west bank of the Feather River. The town of Oroville was across the river. The hotel sat on a steep riverbank 80 feet high. It was a prominent site for everyone to see. To this point, $20,000 had been used in the construction of the hotel. The total cost to complete the building was near $36,000. The plastering had not yet been accomplished. There were 62 rooms. The project had come to a standstill and was being offered to the Odd Fellows as a "free gift." Of course, there was an encumbrance of $3,000 still owed against the project by the developers. The Odd Fellows would have had to pay this amount if it accepted the gift.

When the people of Oroville heard this would become a home for the Odd Fellows, they stepped forward and offered to pay the $3,000 so the gift would be "entirely free." According to the report of the trustees, the owners also made an offer that would allow the Odd Fellows to purchase an "additional one hundred acres of Colony land on the citrus bearing plain, with water for the same, at fifty dollars per acre," if so desired. The option also included another 10 acres of river-bottom land at the foot of the bluff. This would prove to be beneficial in later years, as this region was not only known for citrus but gold mining as well.

In coming years, the Odd Fellows would purchase the additional acreage for the stipulated "fifty dollars per acre."

SUPPLEMENT TO THE OROVILLE REGISTER, APRIL 26, 1899.

AN ADDRESS

TO THE

Members of the Grand Lodge, I. O. O. F.

OF THE

STATE OF CALIFORNIA

ON THE

ODD FELLOWS' HOME.

At a regular meeting of Oroville Lodge No. 59, I. O. O. F., held April 17, 1899, the following resolution was unanimously adopted:

"*Resolved*, That a Committee of five be appointed by the N. G. to take such steps as may be necessary in order to present the actual facts concerning the present Odd Fellows' Home, to the members of the next Grand Lodge, and that such Committee be empowered to appoint such Sub-Committees as they may consider necessary."

In accordance with this resolution the N. G. appointed the following Committee, all of whom are Past Grands, viz: W. E. Duncan, Jr., E. J. Mitchell, Joe Marks, S. S. Simon and Max Marks.

Reason for Such Action.

The appointment of this Committee is the outgrowth of a full and ample discussion at several meetings of the Lodge of the majority report of the Special Committee on the Odd Fellows' Home.

To those familiar with the situation such majority report is so far at variance, in many material matters, with the facts, as to tax to the utmost our confidence in the intention of such majority. Even

The above is the front page of a report that was instigated and written by the members of Oroville Lodge No. 59, who sought to respond to all criticisms made of the Thermalito Odd Fellows Home. In 1899, it appeared in the *Oroville Register*.

Two residents sitting on the railing. Notice the orange groves in the background.

CHAPTER 5

THERMALITO IS SELECTED

O n December 11, 1894, in San Francisco, less than 3 weeks after visiting Thermalito, the board voted to accept the "free gift" by a vote of four to one. On January 26, 1895, the Odd Fellows received the title to the property. The Odd Fellows had its long-awaited home.

The home was designated in the Deed of Endowment to be established as a "Home for Aged and Indigent Odd Fellows, their Wives,

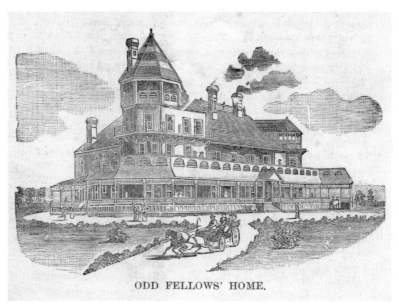

ODD FELLOWS' HOME.

A rendering of the Odd Fellows home, which was on the last page of the 1899 Oroville Lodge report.

Widows and Orphans." The grant deed was very descriptive as to where the property and future offers of property were located. The terms were laid out very clearly and in the favor of the Odd Fellows. The document was finally notarized by a local Butte County, California, notary, John P. Leonard.

Before the trustees had accepted the property, it consulted members of the State Board of Health and the State Medical Society. The trustees reported the following:

> "... the site was one of the most healthful that could be selected within the borders of the State. The atmosphere at this point carries less moisture than at any other which had come under our observation, and less than will be found at any other place within the State outside of the foothills of the Sierras."

The report of the trustees was lengthy and only commended the new site for its tremendous health advantages and agricultural potential.

Other key members were brought to the property to inspect the structure and the grounds. The Odd Fellows immediately took bids in order to complete the building project where the Colony Association had left off. The trustees also decided to include electricity in the new home as it was considered safer to use than oil. They added fruit trees, ornamental shrubs, and flowering plants to the landscape. They cleared off the river-bottom land and obtained wood for later use. Mrs. Jones, the wife of Albert F. Jones, donated 36 trees to enhance the property, for which the board members were thankful.

In addition to concerning itself with providing a home for the older and infirmed members of the Order, the trustees realistically conceded with the Rebekahs that orphaned children could not be in the same facility as the older members. In fact, at their session of 1894, the Rebekahs had appointed a Committee of Conference to discuss that very matter. The trustees assured the Rebekahs that the money donated by the Rebekah Lodges toward the home in Thermalito would be designated for a separate home for the orphans. Caring for the orphans was the primary goal of the Rebekahs.

The trustees had planned to secure a building on the Thermalito land to house orphans. In its lengthy report of 1895, the trustees included this statement:

> "We recognize the fact that the orphans of the Order should be cared for in a separate building from that devoted to the care of the aged and infirm, and have already expended considerable more money than that which has been received from the Rebekah Lodges in securing such a building and one well adapted to that use. If in the future it shall prove too small for the purpose, it may be added to or a new and larger one built in the immediate vicinity of the present Home, and we shall at times be happy to receive the aid of our sisters of the degree of Rebekah through such representatives as their convention may appoint, not only in providing the Home, but in the government and management thereof. Miss Benjamin, one of their committee, has personally inspected the Home and every place examined in the south, and expressed herself highly pleased with the selection made and the work done."

Time would give the Odd Fellows and Rebekahs another location in which to place the home for the orphans. It was not going to be in Thermalito.

In short time, the trustees would dissect and redefine the phrase, "For Aged and Indigent Odd Fellows, their Wives and Orphans." They concluded this title was too broad. It was determined that to be admitted into the home, one would have to reside in California, be a member of the Order, be a wife, widow, or orphan of a member, indigent and unable to earn a living, or suffer from a disease brought on by age.

The lodges also needed questions answered. Most lodges of this time period paid sick benefits to members who fell ill and required assistance from these lodges. If a member who was receiving such a benefit was admitted to the home, would he still be eligible for this financial benefit? These kinds of concerns were being brought to the Grand Lodge. There were also old members who were not indigent and without families who wanted admission to the home, and were willing to pay to stay for the remainder of their lives. Would these members be allowed to live in the home? If so, what would they be charged for living there?

The trustees then searched for a superintendent of the home, and A. L. Bartlett, a member of Riverside Lodge No. 282, was selected. His wife Mabel Bartlett, a Rebekah, was selected as the matron of the home. The trustees were confident in the Bartletts' abilities. They were given residency on the property in temporary quarters on March 1, 1895.

The home was not yet opened, but applications for admission were being sent to the trustees for their consideration and evaluation. Of those, Mr. Williams, a member of San Francisco Lodge No. 3, who was about 80 years old and a member of the Odd Fellows for 43 years, had begged for immediate admission. The trustees were so convinced of his need that he was allowed admittance and housed with the superintendent and matron in the temporary quarters. Mr. Williams became the first "inmate" of the Thermalito Odd Fellows Home. He was so appreciative to be allowed admittance into the home that he brought with him "two hundred grape vines, which he has planted upon the grounds, and hoped to eat fruit from the vines planted by his own hands."

On April 26, 1895, on the anniversary of the Order, the home, though not quite completed, was dedicated. The home was slated to be opened on July 1, 1895.

There was a large celebration to recognize the new Odd Fellows home. On April 4, 1895, prior to the dedication, the following article was printed in the *Oroville Register*:

> "The parade will be the largest ever seen here, being composed of military and civic societies from different parts of the state will march through principle parts of the town to the court house where the literary exercises will be held. The Governor and his staff will be in attendance."

At this period of California history, the Odd Fellows was one of the most influential organizations in the state. Events were always well attended by large audiences, by members and nonmembers alike.

One of the first images of the home. There were many events held at the home. The citizens of Oroville often attended these events, circa 1896. (Courtesy of CSU, Chico, Meriam Library Special Collections, Mildred Forester, Cat# Sc26461.)

Before the home opened, the trustees thanked the following persons:

The citizens of Oroville for paying the outstanding debts of the previous owners in order to conclude the deal.

Member C. C. Terrill, the supervising architect, who took no compensation.

Senator Shippey, for the gift of a valuable cow.

Member George Cordy, for two valuable pigs.

F. E. Paul, for a valuable pig and a number of fowl.

George Ditzlet, for forty "Umbrella" trees and a hundred asparagus roots.

And to the many other donors who gave just about everything imaginable for agricultural and farming needs.

By the end of the 1895 Grand Lodge Annual Session, several decisions had been made concerning questions that had been asked earlier. Of these, it was concluded that elderly members who wished to reside at the home, not being indigent, could stay on a month-to-month basis for a fee determined by the trustees. It was also determined

John H. Simpson was the Grand Master when Thermalito was chosen as the site of the new I.O.O.F. home in 1895.

no members admitted to the home would be entitled to sick benefits (payments) or funeral benefits if he should die; however, if his lodge's by-laws allowed funeral benefits, such payment would be transferred into the Odd Fellows' Home Fund if he was buried by the home. No member while an inmate of the home would be required to pay dues. Orphans or half-orphans of Odd Fellows under the age of 14 years of age, without a home of suitable means, "may be admitted and cared for in the Home at Thermalito."

It was stated in the rules: "This Home is not founded and is not to be used as a Hospital for the care of persons temporarily disabled by sickness or accident." Rules were established and guidelines laid out for everyone to read and understand. None were too difficult to understand.

Several months after visiting the proposed site on November 24, 1894, the trustees had achieved their mission and established an Odd Fellows home in California. Thermalito was to become a place in Odd Fellows' history.

CHAPTER 6

MOVING TOWARD THE HOME OPERATION

The first item of business conducted by the trustees, who oversaw the operations at the new Odd Fellows home, was the numerous acknowledgements and appreciation to everyone that contributed to the establishment.

The money given by the Odd Fellows subordinate lodges totaled $15,866.20. Nearly this entire amount was placed toward the

A very early photograph of the Odd Fellows home, ca. 1897. (Courtesy of CSU, Chico, Meriam Library Special Collections, Pioneer Memorial Museum, cat# Sc21220.)

completion of the building and the related construction costs. Enterprise Lodge No. 298 gave a property that it purchased for $150 to the home board for the sole purpose of it becoming an orphans' home. This land was located very close to the new Odd Fellows home. In the meantime, until a building could be erected for an orphans' home, a small cottage next to the new home would be temporarily used to house orphans.

The Rebekah Lodges gave a total of $1,750.10. It was agreed and understood that the money given by the Rebekahs would be designated for an orphans' home. After all, this became the primary purpose of the women as the creation of an orphans' home was the focus of their annual assembly meetings.

Of course, other donations were made by other factions of the Order. The Encampments gave money, the Veteran Odd Fellows' Association gave money, and individuals gave money; the year-end total was a whopping $38,797.50. It was evident the Order was determined to have this new home. The 1896 report submitted by the trustees supported the need for the donated money, as $32,133.82 was used to put the home in operation.

An abundance of other donations came in the form of furniture, trees, and free medicinal items for one month from the Oroville Drug Store, and a library consisting of shelving and 4,000 volumes was provided by the Odd Fellows' Library Association of Sacramento. All of these things made a home.

A concern that kept coming to the trustees was that of the orphans' home. The Rebekah Assembly had informed the trustees of the home that an entirely different site would be required for an orphans' home, and the Assembly would make a "strong effort" to see that the two homes were separate and that the operations of an orphans' home would be entirely under the control of the Rebekah Branch of the Order. The trustees of the Odd Fellows' home thought such a move would be "ill advised." It was important to the Rebekahs that the money donated toward the home project be made available for an orphans' home.

On May 13, 1896, the Rebekah Assembly was so concerned about the future location of an orphans' home, that it appointed a special committee for this purpose and requested a meeting with representatives of the Grand Lodge that very evening at 7:30 p.m. in the Grand Secretary's office. They met and the Grand Lodge subsequently voted and gave approval to the Rebekahs that they would locate and maintain an orphans' home away from the Odd Fellows home.

With the donations and the construction on the main building completed, the home was in full operation. Applications were received from all over the state. Seventy-nine applicants were approved. These, of course, were indigent "brothers and sisters" of the Order. Sixty-nine of these were admitted to the home by the time the trustees gave their report in 1896.

One applicant was Maria Eva Hoy, a 63-year-old blind lady (widow of a member). Had she been indigent, she would have been eligible for admittance. However, she possessed certain assets. She owned a house and a lot in Alameda, which had cost over $6,000, and she had a mortgage of $2,000 that was still owed.

"At her own suggestions and request, transferred said property to Brother Chas N. Fox, as trustee, in trust to sell the same, pay off the

Residents on the front porch of the home.

mortgage and two or three hundred dollars of floating indebtedness, and out of the balance of the proceeds pay the Odd Fellow's Home Fund a thousand dollars for a life membership for her, and requested that she be admitted at once to the Home."

Of these 79 qualified persons approved to take residence at the home in the first year, one member was deemed "insane" upon his arrival and left the next day, and within a few days, he was admitted to an insane asylum. Another had come directly from an asylum to the home and was considered to be "manifestly insane." He grew worse from day to day and was described as "becoming dangerous" and was a threat to the other inmates. The resident director had the man transferred and committed to an asylum in Napa, California. The man died 2 weeks later, and his body was returned to the Odd Fellows home in Thermalito, where he was buried in the home cemetery. The death of this man caused so great a concern to yet another resident at the home, who suffered from "brain trouble," fearing he would be sent to an asylum, he and his wife left the home. A few others had been disqualified after discovering they had financial means or were not incapacitated as

Residents enjoying the outdoor air on the side porch.

first thought. Four of the inmates died. That left 52 indigent and three life members at the home.

The trustees also reported that all of the residents ("inmates," as they were called) were "in better health than when they arrived." There were rules set in place, too. None of the residents were allowed to leave without permission. All were required to be courteous towards each other, and all must follow a "rigid insistence upon personal cleanliness."

The five trustees who signed the 1896 report were: Charles N. Fox, William H. Barnes, S. B. Smith, Fred J. Moll, Sr. (the member who, in 1892, submitted a resolution that caused the Grand Lodge to move quicker toward establishing a home), and Albert F. Joes, the man who offered the Thermalito property, including the unfinished Bella Vista Hotel.

The Odd Fellows home in Thermalito may have been in full operation, but a Special Committee was appointed to conduct an investigation of it.

CHAPTER 7

EXPANSION OF THERMALITO, CALIFORNIA

T hermalito is located in Butte County, one of the first counties created in 1850, which had been reduced in size several times before Thermalito became a town. The name "Thermalito" is related to "little hot spring," which originated from the Greek word "thermae." Today, Thermalito is also referred to as the "Forebay" or "Afterbay," depending on the point of reference. These names were derived after the construction of the Oroville Dam, which had caused these two areas of water to form in the Thermalito vicinity.

In her book, *Old Days in Butte*, Florence Danforth Boyle states that Thermalito was developed because there was a "need for farm

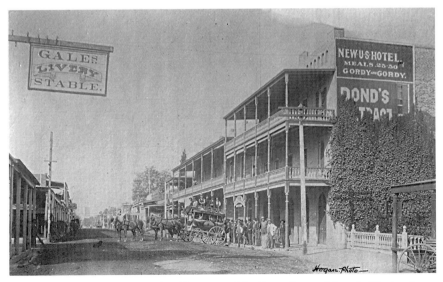

An early photo of Oroville. (Courtesy of the Butte County Historical Society.)

Seen here, Edward W. Fogg was a donor of the Bella Vista Hotel. He continued to success-fully produce olives and olive oil. (Courtesy of CSU, Chico, Meriam Library Special Collections, Pioneer Memorial Museum, cat# Sc21217.)

production." Up until the 1880s, most of the region in that area of Butte County was primarily used for mining operations. The town of Oroville sat just across the Feather River, and this is where literally tons of gold were taken from dredging the river bottom. Mining gold was the chief concern of any person living in this area.

In the 1880s, Major Frank McLaughlin, Edward W. Fogg, and Albert F. Jones, each from Oroville, bought an old Miocene ditch system, which had been used to bring water to the area's mines. They bought 8,000 acres, which would later be used to grow oranges. These men had aspirations of becoming the largest citrus and olive growers in the state. They created the Thermalito Citrus Colony.

On February 11, 1886, a meeting was held in the Oroville Court-house where the Thermalito Citrus Colony secured the financial investment of $20,000 from 20 of the town's businessmen. This was an investment in agriculture and the production of oranges and olives. Five years later (1891), the Oroville City Association entered samples of the oranges grown in Thermalito in the State Citrus Fair, held in Marysville.

Major Frank McLaughlin (far left), a principle figure in the Thermalito Colony Company, was one of three men to donate the Bella Vista Hotel and its surrounding lands. He was also a member of the Odd Fellows. (Courtesy of the Butte County Historical Society.)

Odd Fellow and successful businessman Albert F. Jones was one of three men who donated the not-yet completed Bella Vista Hotel to the Odd Fellows for its future home. He eventually became one of its trustees.

It was decided that the best oranges presented at the fair were those grown in Thermalito. In fact, from then on, oranges from Thermalito were always rated as one of the best at fairs throughout the state.

The Thermalito Citrus Colony now called itself the Thermalito Land Colony. It was venturing out to expand Thermalito beyond a place of just orange groves. In 1888, the group broke ground for a resort hotel. The group sought to bring people into the surrounding areas of Thermalito by also selling acres of land from $50 to $150 per acre.

On February 4, 1889, an advertisement in the Monday evening newspaper read: "THERMALITO'S MARVELOUS PROGRESS OF THE BEAUTIFUL COLONY OF CENTRAL CALIFORNIA." Of course, the

The caption for this early photograph at the home reads, "Little German Band and Orange Trees."

advertisement listed the acres for sale. It also boasted the "Bella Vista Hotel, Largest Hotel in California North of Sacramento." The company was now called the Thermalito Colony Company.

The summer heat was blamed for the lack of sales. The expectations of the Colony fell short of anything resembling a success. The owners were stuck with a $3,000 debt for the hotel's construction and could not proceed with finishing the project. In November of 1894, Albert F. Jones, the president of the Colony, met with the Odd Fellows to offer it the hotel and surrounding lands free of charge. Mr. Jones and his associate, Major McLaughlin, were members already of the Odd Fellows and thought this could be a perfect deal. The only condition was that the $3,000 debt had to be paid off, in which the good citizens of Oroville who had supported the idea of an Odd Fellows home in Thermalito gladly paid.

In the years to come, the town of Thermalito grew from the eventual expansion of the Odd Fellows home. And, after the relocation of the home in 1912, other various "colonies," or land deals, would be offered. Thermalito would continue to grow.

A front and east side view of the home.

CHAPTER 8

THE HOME'S FACTS AS REPORTED

B y mid-1897, the home had expanded its size acreage to about 85 acres. It had also established a cemetery and added various buildings to the home's grounds. It now had one 108 residents. However, one inmate was found to be receiving a government pension and had already been at a home for life in a soldiers' home. Therefore, he was informed he could not stay and was returned to the home provided by the government. There were others that left on their own, or were taken away to asylums, or died, that reduced the total number from 108 to 79 (70 brothers and nine sisters).

Residents relaxing in the sitting room.

Aside from the natural occurrences of elderly inmates dying, the reports from the trustees came in as positive. The trustees defended the location of the home by stating "not a single death at the Home has been from local causes. Trustees were always ready to offer an explanation for

Grand Master Perley S. Gosbey, 1896. He supported and reappointed a Special Committee to oversee the operations at the home.

those outside complaints or suspicions, and there had been a few. To balance these complaints, Grand Master Perley S. Gosbey appointed a
Special Committee on the I.O.O.F. Home to conduct an investigation of
the home, its practices, its employees, and its overall operation. The
Special Committee was concerned about the trustees' acquisition of
additional properties around the home without the approval of the
Grand Body. The investigative committee included five members."

Since the annual meeting of the Grand Lodge in 1896, the
trustees had bought four more lots. One of these lots had a barn. Two
more lots were donated, one by Trustee Albert F. Jones, and the other
by John P. Irish, Esq. In addition to these said lots, the trustees purchased another 35 acres of Colony lands. Of course, the plan was to
cultivate the land to grow "citrus, fruits, and olives." The home was
now comprised of 75 acres of land. This did not include the land to be

An 1897 Christmas photograph of the residents standing in front of the home. (California
Historical Society, FN-12913.)

used as the cemetery. A part of this land had been donated and another purchased by the trustees. The cemetery was named "Patriarchs' Rest." This would be put to use soon enough.

The trustees also added an additional annex of 40 rooms to the home. A building was built for doing the laundry, a storehouse for hay was constructed, a room was added onto the newly purchased barn, and other outbuildings and a cow stable were also built. Still, many donations of items for use at the home were coming in all of the time. So many items came in that the trustees said the list "is too long for publication"; however, many items, mostly farm animals, furniture, and tools, were reported. The home and the property was valued at $60,000, with no liabilities.

It should be mentioned that the Odd Fellows, as a group, favored employment from within the Order. The home was required to first offer positions of employment at the home to members. The laundry work seemed to place the trustees in a defensible position:

> "In the laundry the Superintendent and members of the Board have all made strenuous efforts to secure Odd Fellows for the work, but after several trials we have been unable to find either Odd Fellows, or white persons who were not Odd Fellows, who could and would do the work, in view of its quantity and character. An average of about six thousand pieces per month pass through our laundry and every day more or less of these pieces, sometimes as high as a dozen or fifteen per day are from the beds or bodies of helpless invalids, and of a character such as every white person we have yet tried refuses to handle. For this reason, and this alone, our laundry, which is in a separate building, is in charge of Chinese."

The trustees also decided to hire A. L. Bartlett as the permanent superintendent of the home and his wife as the matron, reporting that this decision had also been endorsed by the residents of the home, "save a few isolated cases."

In its final sentence of the trustees' annual report, it recommended an assessment of 50 cents per capita upon the membership in the jurisdiction. This was to be used for the maintenance of the home for the next year.

Chinese parade in downtown Oroville, 1905. Several workers from this community provided the laundry service at the home, but were later replaced because of racism. (Courtesy of CSU, Chico, Meriam Library Special Collections, John Nopel Collection, cat# Sc50172.)

An employee of the home. (Courtesy of the Butte Historical Society.)

The report by the trustees in 1897 contained so many unanswered questions that Grand Master John Warboys appointed the Special Committee on the I.O.O.F. Home, which was to investigate the practices at the home. The report of the trustees was submitted on May 11, 1897. On May 14, 1897, the Special Committee left San Francisco for the Thermalito Home to conduct an investigation.

Grand Master John W. Warboys, 1897.

CHAPTER 9

A NEGATIVE REPORT

The Special Committee on the I.O.O.F. Home arrived at the home at twelve o'clock midnight and began interviewing witnesses at five o'clock the following morning. The committee stated that 80 witnesses at the home were examined and another 20 from the town. Three stenographers were hired to speed the process of the interviews.

The investigation committee had found and reported the buildings were in good condition and the grounds were excellent, but "earnestly protest against the purchase of any more land in Thermalito."

They found the buildings to be constructed of light and inflammable materials, without protection from fire. They suggested bringing a water source closer to the buildings and to conduct fire drills.

The investigation committee found there was a need for an assistant cook. The graves at the Patriarchs' Cemetery, or "Patriarchs' Rest," as the committee called it, needed to have inexpensive monuments inscribed with the proper information. It found many members at the home should not have been admitted because they were sick before they arrived and that their subordinate lodges should have been caring for them and giving them sick benefits. The policy was not to admit members who were sick. The home was not a hospital.

The investigation committee suggested certain portions of land should be used for planting vegetables and to permit the inmates to tend to this task if they wish.

Concerning the laundry work, the committee made these remarks:

> "Our attention has been especially directed to the laundry, which is at the present time conducted entirely by Chinese at a wage expense of about $87.50 per month. There seems to be no good reason why, in a Home supported by a fraternal and philanthropic organization, such an important feature should be in the hands of an element so entirely at variance with the feelings of all those members of the Home, and we earnestly recommend that white labor be employed at the earliest possible moment, and thereafter be continued in and about the Home. Members of the Order should be employed where assistance is necessary, and in no case should Asiatic labor be employed in or about the Home."

It is as if the Special Committee on the I.O.O.F. Home ignored the previous explanation given by the trustees of the home. There are indications by these two conflicting reports that a division might exist between members of the Grand Lodge concerning the home. It seems the members who were slow to provide a home in the 1880s were now exacting retribution on the members who pursued the idea of establishing one. Even the Rebekah Assembly was opposed to the home because it saw the trustees dictating that the orphans' home should be situated on the grounds next the home in Thermalito. There was opposition to having the home, and this kind of "special investigation" was to prove this fact.

Finally, the investigation committee looked at the treatment of the inmates. It stated that in the testimonies of all of the inmates, also all of the employees, and others who had been formerly employed, that 50 percent of the inmates complained of their treatment by the superintendent.

Also, this report by the investigating committee is in conflict with the home trustees, who had reported that the inmates approved of the superintendent, thus the reason cited for hiring the superintendent and his wife, the matron. But the investigating committee was not yet finished with this part of the investigation.

The inmates complained that the superintendent was "cold and unsympathetic." They said that he was "high-tempered and overbearing," and was causing disharmony in the home. The committee recommended that a new superintendent be employed. In addition to recommending the superintendent be replaced, the committee suggested the physician, matron, and nurse be replaced as well. Until that time, the inmates could not trust the care they were receiving.

The result of this report showed that a definite division of opinions and observations existed amongst the ranks of the membership. From 1898 on, the Grand Masters kept the balance by including the home, and the condition thereof, in their annual reports. It was important the Grand Master knew what was happening at the facility at all times. It was visited by these Grand Masters sometimes without warning. The home, in itself, was a credit to the honor of the Order, but the politics probably never afforded Thermalito the opportunity to remain its permanent site.

CHAPTER 10

LIFE AT THE THERMALITO HOME AS REPORTED

Much of the following information was taken from the annual reports of the trustees of the Odd Fellows home. After the 1897 report of the investigating committee, the reports became detailed and extremely worded. There was minimal information excluded from these reports, except in a few circumstances, which would later be revealed. Of all of the reports given on the Odd Fellows Home in Thermalito by the Grand Masters (there was a new one elected each year for the jurisdiction), the report given in 1898 by Grand Master A. M. Drew was the most detailed; it was several pages long. In the following years, the reports given by these Grand Masters were not longer than a paragraph or two.

Grand Master A. M. Drew visited the home on November 7, 1897, and April 8, 1898. He met the new Superintendent Frederick J. Moll, Sr.—the same member that had pushed the Grand Lodge into establishing a home for the Odd Fellows back in 1892. Of course, he had to step down from his position of trustee from the previous year to accept the position of superintendent.

The Grand Master reported the inmates approved of the new superintendent and his wife, the new matron of the facility. A resident, Mr. Peabody, was the resident chief gardener, and was doing a good job. The Grand Master also thought the grounds were beautiful and approved of the new doctor. He did have some recommendations: some of the buildings needed painting; an additional acre should be purchased for the livestock as they were too confined in a small area; the cows needed to have a shelter built for them before the winter; and that a better grade of cows be purchased as the ones on hand were inferior.

In 1892, Frederick J. Moll, Sr., demanded the Grand Lodge quit delaying the establishment of a home. He later became a trustee of the home.

The barn, circa 1907. (right)

The hog farm.

Hogs at the farm.

The Grand Master was in Thermalito to make an observation on behalf of the Order, as seen in this report. He was to observe the welfare of the inmates. Future Grand Masters would have this same obligation.

Front of the chicken ranch at the home.

The chicken yard.

In April, 1898, the Home had 81 males and 10 females. The average age was "sixty-eight and one-third years." Grand Master Drew found the residents happy and contented. Several of the residents were helping with the work. There was also mention of another attitude coming from some of the older gentlemen described as being

The chicken yard and a woodpile.

The chicken yard in 1909.

fault-finding and discontented, and "from a natural disposition, be unhappy in any condition in life."

The Grand Master also suggested steam heaters be installed in the rooms and that another addition be built to accommodate more future

Look at all the chicken coops!

The brooding yard.

residents. He added that all water use for domestic purposes be distilled so that all "malarial symptoms would disappear." Up to this time, there had been no such mention of malaria; however, this will become a major issue in the coming years.

In 1898, Grand Master Alexander M. Drew recommended the home use distilled water to reduce the symptoms of malaria. This was the first time "malaria" had ever been mentioned concerning the home. Malaria would later become the major point in the arguments to move the site.

After the 1897 report by the Special Committee on the I.O.O.F. Home, the trustees had to remove the Chinese workers from the laundry. The trustees were forced to purchase an engine along with other

The laundry room. Notice the belt drives the motor. This motorized method reduced the number of laborers needed to wash the laundry.

Another view of the laundry room.

machinery to operate the new laundry system. It cost $800 for the new equipment.

The trustees were also compelled to repay the Rebekahs the donations that were made toward the orphans' home. The Rebekah Assembly stood its ground on having an orphans' home separate from

William Quayle was once the oldest resident (circa 1899).

a home for aged members, and finally constructed an orphans' home in Gilroy, California. It was dedicated on October 27, 1897.

On a less business-related note, Farnsworth Lodge No. 95 presented a glorious flag to the I.O.O.F. Home. The flag was 13-by-25 feet. This was a special event. On April 9, 1898, resident and long-time member of the Order, William Quayle, unfolded the large flag and raised it into the air. The crowd who witnessed this event cheered and later celebrated in the evening when members shared stories of the late Past Grand Sire Farnsworth, and how this man worked to reconcile those who had fought against each other in the

James F. Thompson was the Grand Master in 1898.

Civil War and to bring these brothers back to the three-links (the symbol of Odd Fellowship).

In 1846, William Quayle was with Commodore John D. Sloat, when Sloat led the navy into battle. Sloat was victorious in the "Battle of Monterey," where he proclaimed California as part of the United States. At the time Quayle raised the flag at the home, he had been a member for 62 years, having joined the Odd Fellows in 1836. In addition to raising the flag at the home, he had also raised the flag at Monterey in 1846. Quayle was one of several veterans at the home who received a $12 monthly pension from the United States government. He regularly donated his money to the home.

In the trustees' report of 1898, 10 more members had died since 1897; they also stated "those who have so far come are the relics of forty years of growth of the Order in this State, and very many of them have reached the Home in apparently a dying condition."

The resident physician reported several cases of malaria. The trustees were confident the cases of malaria would decrease or disappear completely by the next reporting period, because they reasoned, the malaria had been brought about by the tilling and exposing of fresh earth with water and sun.

By May of 1898, the home found itself unable to keep up with the bills, partly blaming the situation on having to purchase the new laundry machine, which replaced the Chinese labor. It was also ordered to repay the Rebekahs Assembly the money that had been donated toward the construction of an orphan's home.

Most of the following images were taken in 1907 from the *Annual Journals* (notice the palm motif).

Various views of the home happenings.

Photos with orange motif.

Photos with orange motif.

Note the California poppy motif.

Note the daisy motif.

1907.

1907.

CHAPTER 11

RESPONSE TO CRITICISM

Trustee Charles N. Fox responded to all of the criticisms of the membership on behalf of the board. Some of the following complaints had been brought up in the previous sections and seemed to be a reoccurring theme that subtly divided the trustees against the membership.

In response to members who voiced concerns over the location of the home, the trustees simply cited the Grand Lodge's inability to secure a home over a long period of years because there had been so much disagreement about where a facility should be located. The trustees reminded everyone that it was its board that established a home within two years after being assigned the task. The board accomplished its mission—period.

Hot weather was a complaint of many members who did not reside at the home. The trustees said the climate "adapted to the weakened lungs and the sluggish blood of age; to avoid the fogs and cold winds of the sea coast, and find a temperature that was warm and an atmosphere that was dry and pure."

Odd Fellows were concerned about the health of the residents of the home, citing the number of deaths and developed illnesses at the facility. Again, the trustees offered an answer to these most trying questions: "It is almost a universal rule that those who are not in the last stages of decrepitude or disease very soon commence and, unless set back by some indiscretion on their own part, steadily continue to improve in physical health until old age itself stops the beating of the heart."

Charles Nelson Fox was the first president of home board.
He staved off many of the verbal attacks on the operation and
existence of the home.

There were complaints about the purchase of additional lands, which were considered useless. The trustees answered by stating the following: "It may not be adapted to all uses. Little, if any, of all the most valuable lands are so adapted. We have not had the means to bring our lands under cultivation as rapidly as we desired. . ."

The membership complained of the way some titles to the home properties had been acquired. The trustee stated, "As to the title itself I need only say: The title to every inch of land is founded upon Mexican Grant, confirmed by the Courts and patented by the Government of the United States, and has come down to us by a regular chain of conveyances, and is free from encumbrance." The land was

582   JOURNAL OF PROCEEDINGS OF THE   [1899.

JULY, 1898.

Day of Month.	Maximum.	Minimum.	Range.	Prevailing Direction of Wind.	Character of Day.	Summary of Month.
1	100	80	20	S. E.	Clear	
2	104	86	18	"	"	
3	102	76	96	"	"	
4	98	70	28	"	"	
5	98	76	22	"	"	
6	94	74	20	"	"	
7	94	74	20	"	"	
8	94	76	18	"	"	
9	92	68	24	"	"	
10	92	62	30	"	"	
11	98	60	38	"	"	Temperature.
12	98	60	38	"	"	Mean Maximum ... 98
13	94	62	32	N. W.	"	Mean Minimum ... 72
14	98	68	30	S.S.E.	"	Mean............. 85
15	98	74	24	S.	"	Maximum.........110
16	92	72	20	"	"	Date, 29th.
17	94	72	22	"	"	Minimum...... 60
18	100	76	24	"	"	Dates, 11, 12, 21.
19	100	74	26	S. E.	"	Mean Range....... 26
20	84	68	16	"	"	
21	84	60	24	"	"	
22	90	64	26	"	"	
23	92	70	22	"	"	Character of Days.
24	98	74	24	"	P. C.	Clear...............23
25	104	70	34	"	Smoky	P. C...... 1
26	108	78	30	"	"	Smoky.............7
27	109	76	33	"	"	
28	109	72	37	"	"	
29	110	78	32	"	"	
30	104	78	26	"	"	
31	102	74	28	"	"	
Summary	3034	2222	812			
Mean	98	72	26			

July 18th and 19th—Strong Wind.

1899.]   GRAND LODGE OF CALIFORNIA.   583

AUGUST, 1898.

Day of Month.	Maximum.	Minimum.	Range.	Prevailing Direction of Wind.	Character of Day.	Summary of Month.
1	96	70	26	S. E.	Clear	
2	90	64	22	"	P. C.	
3	92	60	32	"	Clear but	
4	96	72	24	"	Smoky	
5	98	76	22	"	"	
6	94	74	20	"	"	
7	94	74	20	"	"	
8	104	76	28	"	"	
9	106	76	30	"	"	
10	168	80	28	"	"	Temperature.
11	114	82	32	N. W.	"	Mean Maximum 97
12	112	88	24	"	"	Mean Minimum 72
13	108	84	24	"	"	Mean............. 85
14	108	84	24	"	"	Maximum......... 112
15	102	76	26	S. E.	P. C.	Minimum.......... 59
16	98	72	26	"	"	Date, 12th.
17	98	72	26	"	"	Date, 30th.
18	92	76	16	"	Cloudy	Range, Mean....... 26
19	92	74	18	"	Clear	
20	90	60	30	"	"	
21	98	64	34	"	"	
22	98	70	28	"	"	
23	94	72	22	"	"	Character of Days.
24	102	64	38	"	"	Clear............... 7
25	101	70	31	"	"	Clear, but Smoky...12
26	101	68	33	"	P. C.	P. C..............10
27	100	66	34	"	"	Cloudy 2
28	90	68	22	"	"	
29	82	66	16	"	"	
30	88	59	29	"	"	
31	82	64	18	"	"	
Summary	3024	2227	803			
Mean	97	72	26			

Heavy Fires in the Mountains for the Month.

A resident of the home kept a journal of the thermometrical readings. Past Grand Myron C. Close was a voluntary observer and crop correspondent of the U.S. Weather Bureau and the Odd Fellows home. These are readings for the months of July and August of 1898. Note the high temperatures.

also held in the names of the trustees, about which the membership had objections.

The trustees had now praised the Rebekah Assembly for establishing an independent orphans home, away from the elderly home in Thermalito, where only a year earlier it stated the effort as "ill advised."

It was clear the trustees were trying to defend themselves and their decisions concerning the establishment and expansion of the home and its surrounding lands. This board had accomplished in such a short time what many thought was impossible. It is apparent the change of having a home and having to financially support a home had caught the membership off-guard. Perhaps they thought the home would be self-supporting. The board was also at odds with the membership having to defend itself against these criticisms after doing such an impossible job of starting such a facility.

After the board had answered these harsh criticisms, the Special I.O.O.F. Home Committee was once again asked to investigate the home.

CHAPTER 12

MORE CRITICISM

On March 6, 1899, seven lodges from Humboldt County, without any proper authority according to the Grand Lodge, submitted a letter that basically disapproved of the proposed assessments on lodges for the support of the home.

Two years earlier, these lodges of Humboldt County had sent a similar letter complaining of the home.

Both of these letters were without the approval of the Grand Master and considered illegal under the laws of the Order. The letters had been sent to all of the subordinate lodges in the state.

These seven lodges had echoed some of the feelings of many Odd Fellows. The following is an excerpt of part of this controversial letter: "That promoters erred in their estimate of maintaining the Home in its location cannot be denied. That the lodges of the State are unable to no longer stand the expensive drain on their funds is also a matter past dispute." The Grand Lodge, which was obligated to enforce the strict laws of the Order, stepped in to denounce this argumentative letter. There were rules, and they needed to be followed. But the damage was already done. The lodges had read the letter sent by the Humboldt lodges. How could they have ignored the letter?

On April 23, 1899, Grand Master Karl C. Brueck visited the home at Thermalito. This was a surprise visit. His report was not lengthy, but his most serious complaint was that no prayer was "offered" at the meals, nor had religious services been conducted.

The Special I.O.O.F. Home Committee was sent to Thermalito to make a full investigation again. Without going into detail, because

During his visit in 1899, Karl C. Brueck complained the residents were not saying grace before the meals.

it would only echo the investigation of the previous year, the conclusion and level of criticism was the same in the investigation. Then again, the location of the home seemed to be the main concern of this committee. While the lodges were complaining about having to pay assessments for the facility, the committee was addressing location in more than one way. First, the committee reported the actual location:

> "The Home is located in the Sacramento Valley at a settlement called Thermalito, one hundred and fifty miles northeast of San Fran cisco, and one mile in an air line west of the town of Oroville, at an altitude of two hundred and forty feet above sea level and eighty feet above the Feather River."

Then it reported indirectly on matters that would affect the location of the facility in Thermalito by stating:

> "No restrictions were placed in the deed as to where such a Home should be located, and no reversion was saved in case the Home was located elsewhere, or moved after having been located thereon; the legal effect of this conveyance is to make the property trust property, the use, income, or proceeds thereof to be devoted exclusively to the purpose of the trust. Hence we, as an Order, are under no legal obligations to maintain the Home at Thermalito."

Finally, it hammered the proverbial nail into the coffin: "While we believe the location was an unfortunate one, a reference to the authority of the committee charged with the location will show they were expected to get something for nothing." The committee suggested a new site be purchased for the construction of a new home.

Malaria was an issue again addressed in the committee's report. In a 9-month period, there were 97 cases of malaria. Even the staff suffered malaria. Doctor Kusel, the home's doctor, during his testimony to the committee, said the location of the home was "malarious."

Heat was another factor damning the location. The residents complained constantly of the heat according to the report. They could not sleep at night. August and September were very hot months. On January 9, 1899, the resident doctor before Dr. Kusel wrote: ". . .I cannot too strongly condemn Thermalito as a location for the Home for Aged of the Order. The fact is in great evidence that the heat during the summer months is simply unbearable." He went on to complain about

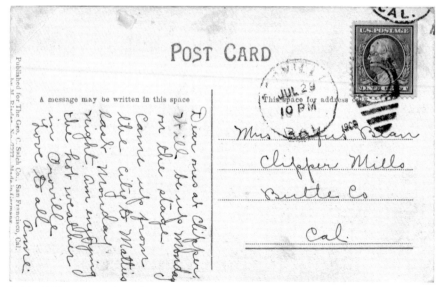

A July 1909 postcard from Oroville, which mentions the "hot weather." The actual photograph was taken prior to 1899.

A pot of calla lilies on the porch of the hospital. Pillows and wicker chairs are arranged to make the inmates comfortable.

malaria, saying that he had treated at least everyone at the home at least one time for this affliction.

There was a Minority Report offered as well. It did not contradict what the majority of the committee reported, other than citing the many improvements that had been done to the property and how well the operation of the home was handled. Minority Reports were common, as these reports offered those individual committee members, who disagreed with the majority, an opportunity to support such disagreements with written reports.

Finally the trustees of the facility made their report to the Grand Lodge. It was no surprise that after the reporting of the facts, happenings, and year-end financials, that the tone of the report would be somewhat defensive. The Grand Master found criticism; the Special I.O.O.F. Home Committee found criticism; and various lodges throughout the state had found criticism of the home.

The home had only been opened a few years now. It was still in its infancy. This early criticism, which appears more like a barrage of attacks on an evolving Odd Fellows ideology and where the Order houses the needy segment of its membership, would eventually win out. But, because of the consistent, positive, responsive reports offered by the trustees year after year, only reporting the facts and always answering the criticisms, the home lasted year after year. It had brave defenders during this period. The board of trustees for the home did its job, even though the names changed throughout the years. There will be a compromise; but there will be a home!

Although the complaints continued against the facility, work and growth at the home still persisted. The kitchen was enlarged, the third story was completed to house additional inmates, fire escapes were added, water pipes placed throughout the newer part of the main structure, linoleum was placed upon the floors, a wood house and blacksmith shop were built, the cow barn improved, new fences had been installed, the rooms had been painted, more trees were planted, and the list went on and on. So work progressed, and the trustees did all they could to respond to the negative reports.

Most of the items contained in the 1899 Report of the Home Trustees were related to earlier reports including labor, wages, and the requirements for admission. But there was an improvement, by which the residents were now being encouraged to help with small chores around the site. This was an "experiment" to have the residents feel they had purpose and to keep them busy. Unskilled work paid 5 cents a day, while skilled work paid a whopping 7 cents! The trustees were skeptical of how the Grand Lodge would view this project.

It appeared the trustees had responded to nearly all of the concerns and complaints in correcting the issue at hand or simply improving upon something to make it better. Although the trustees often responded in a subtle, yet defensive manner, they worked very hard to fix the problems that had been pointed out with regard to the other reports by the Grand Master (Brueck in 1899) and the Special I.O.O.F. Home Committee.

Eight residents passed away during the reporting period. The reports now included a line-by-line report of the various illnesses that occurred in the year. The number of cases and the name of the illness or disease broke down this report. Some of the illnesses included the following:

Heart affections, catarrhal affections of air passages, chronic rheumatic affections, affections of the bladder and prostate, eye diseases, morphinism, paralysis, mental affections, chronic neuralgia, other nervous affections, chronic constipation, other chronic stomach and intestinal diseases, hernia, malaria (there were 115 cases during this reporting period), constipation, diarrhea, dysentery, bronchitis, gastritis, ischiorectal abscess, facial neuralgia, gastroenteritis, stomatitis, lumbago, hemorrhoids, laryngitis, eczema, insomnia, tuberculosis, retention of urine, pneumonia, pleuropneumonia, tonsillitis, diabetes insipidus, burns, cystitis, varicose ulcer, carbuncle, Bright's disease, and intercostal neuralgia.

(Bright's disease was related to disease of the kidney. In 1827, the disease was named after English physician Richard Bright.)

In subsequent years, this list of illnesses would expand to include: asthma, abscesses, bilious and chills, blood poisoning, chills and general debility, consumption, cramps, colic, congestion of the lungs and brain, kidney disease, dyspepsia, erysipelas of the hand, fever, gastritis, general debility, hives, hydrocele, hemorrhage, heart trouble, heat prostration, indigestion, insanity, inflammation of the eyes and bowels, la grippe, obstruction of the bowels, palpitation of the heart, ruptures, rheumatism, sprained ankles, scrofula, sciatica, toe amputations, and varicose veins. Where many of these illnesses changed from year to year, malaria was always present and on the lists.

In 1899, the last request made in the report by the trustees was to be able to build a separate hospital not too far from the home.

CHAPTER 13

THE HOME—THE NEXT FEW YEARS

I n 1899, citing an "overtaxed system" and a decline in health, Superintendent Moll and his wife, the matron, resigned their employment at the Thermalito Home. Thus, another change occurred in the home.

The home in 1899.

J. C. Glidden, a member of Pacific Lodge No. 155 and an inmate of the Thermalito Home, had written a letter to another lodge complaining of Mrs. Moll, the matron. This letter was said to be "offensive." He was suspended from the home for 1 year. The guidelines of the home must have been very strict if one could not voice his or her complaints of those in charge. Of course, the time period was much different and not nearly as tolerant as now. These kinds of incidences lead one to ponder or suspect there may have been reasons other than an "over-taxed system" for someone to leave a job.

Another member, James McCurry of Osceola Lodge No 215, was suspended for 2 months from the home for using improper language. His lodge did not return him to the facility in Thermalito as it thought the trustees had not treated McCurry fairly.

In January of 1899, the trustees elected F. W. Jaeger, a former janitor, as the new superintendent, and his wife, the matron. This was short-lived as yet another superintendent and his wife were hired later in the year. Dr. William M. Hilton and his wife took over the duties at the Thermalito Home.

Doctor William M. Hilton was hired as the superintendent in 1899. He was also a member of Apollo Lodge No. 123, having joined the Odd Fellows in 1873. Dr. Hilton graduated as a Doctor of Medicine from the State University of Iowa, March 5, 1873. He also served in the Civil War.

The trustees of the home now included George H. Morrison, Samuel B. Smith, J. F. Thompson, Albert F. Jones, and David Newell. The latter had been elected the previous year after former Trustee Charles N. Fox responded to the criticism of the Special I.O.O.F. Home Committee with his own written response. Whatever the reason, Fox did not return to the board to serve as a trustee.

Daniel Flint replaced Trustee George H. Morrison, who had died suddenly, August 13, 1900. Morrison had been the president of the board.

The coming years would be extremely important to everyone, especially the residents at the home and the trustees of the home. Those who did not reside at the facility or take a role in operating it sided with the Special I.O.O.F. Home Committee when presented an ultimatum by way of a resolution to the Grand Body.

In 1899, Jennie Hilton, wife of Superintendent Dr. William Hilton, took over duties of home matron.

An 1899 photograph of James F. Thompson, trustee and
Past Grand Master.

"This resolution is presented upon the statement of Brother A. F.
Jones that if the location be given a fair trial under the conditions suggested for five years and the expiration of that time the location be
decided by this Grand Lodge to not be a desirable one on the grounds of
unfavorable climatic conditions, he and other parties of the first part to
the deed of gift hereinbefore referred to quitclaim their reversion to said
property to the Trustees, thus enabling the Trustees to sell said property
and use the proceeds thereof to buy a new site."

This was really a statement indirectly saying that a committee
would be searching for a new site and the Grand Lodge needed to know
the money would be there for such an undertaking. Who would have
ever believed the "climatic conditions" could change in 5 years? It was

Photograph of David Newell, a home trustee.

impossible. Thermalito was always a temporary situation. The Special I.O.O.F. Home Committee was appointed and reappointed every year with a specific purpose to investigate the home. The reports of the committee had never been positive. But still, because of the tenacity of the board of trustees at the home, it survived year after year. How long would this tenacity hold out? No one knew to this point. The Odd Fellows of California had a home for its aged and infirmed members, but always seemed to be searching for another location. Although it is not suggested in any reports, the idea of not knowing if the facility would be relocated must have had an unsettling effect upon the residents.

On May 27, 1899, a quitclaim to the Thermalito property was signed over to the trustees of the home, placing it in escrow until May 12, 1904. The fate of the home would be decided at that time.

In the late-1890s, George H. Morrison was the second president of the home board.

By the time the dust settled at the 1899 Annual Session of the Grand Lodge and after the debating and argumentative reports came onto the floor, the only way the facility at Thermalito would remain was if the malaria was totally eradicated by May of 1904. This meant absolutely no cases of malaria could be present by that time; otherwise, with the quitclaim having been signed and held in escrow on behalf of the Grand Lodge and the trustees of the home, the property would most likely be sold after a new site for the home had been located. In fact, a resolution had been proposed to appoint a committee to search out new properties. It failed, as it was presumptuous.

There had always been failed resolutions during the Annual Sessions to give up the Thermalito property and search for other locations, but the State of Order Committee sent these resolutions back or

Daniel Flint. In 1899, Flint replaced George H. Morrison as trustee.

recommended they be relieved from further consideration. One can only suppose that cooler heads prevailed and time would provide the needed answers.

In 1900, the next visiting Grand Master to the home, Walter A. Bonynge, pointed out a number of concerns. He noticed there was no heating system supplying heat to the rooms of the inmates and that many went to bed while wearing their clothes. He also addressed the summer conditions, though he had not visited the site in the summer, "on about one hundred days the thermometer stands from ninety to one hundred and fourteen degrees in the shade. . ." He mentioned the malaria situation. He said that the ground was so hard, that ". . .even the digging of a grave must be done by the aid of dynamite." He observed the home lacked even one musical instrument and suggested

In 1900, during his visit, Grand Master Walter A. Bonynge expressed a concern about the lack of a heating system in the rooms at the home.

the trustees be allowed to purchase a piano. Finally, his main concern was the isolation of the home; that it was 3 miles from the nearest railroad. He stated that if anyone wanted to visit the location from San Francisco, it would take 2 days travel and cost $9 [by rail], "consequently, it is beyond the means of the ordinary delegate or member of the Order." To the Grand Master, this circumstance of being isolated was worse for the inmates, as old friends or family members were prevented from visiting, leaving them only the "monotony of waiting for the end." Finally, the Grand Master summed it up by saying,

"They feel, as many of them told me with tears in their eyes, that they had been transported beyond the reach of those who were dear to them, with no relief in sight but death."

Despite being directed not to purchase additional property in Thermalito, the trustees disobeyed the Grand Lodge and purchased a lot where the barn was located. The Odd Fellows had not owned it. However, the trustees did sell 20 acres of land 2½ miles from the home, which they had been ordered to sell.

In 1899, the home created a pharmacy where the new superintendent, who now was also a doctor, could mix compounds and manufacture drugs. This would significantly reduce the cost of medicines at the facility.

The home still made significant progress with improvements. Negative reports outside of the trustees of the home were addressed and acted upon. This board has always taken corrective measures to respond to these directives in a positive and constructive mode.

October 17–19, 1899, 44 residents enjoyed a trip to San Francisco to take part in the Golden Jubilee Celebration of the Order. San Francisco was the home of the first lodge in California. It was fitting to have such a 50-year celebration and include every part of the Odd Fellows organization, including the aged members and widows from the Odd Fellows Home of Thermalito. The residents' lodges had sent $10 each to send them to the celebration. The Grand Secretary made arrangements with the railroad to obtain reduced fairs for the members. The superintendent went along for the excursion as well. Trustee David Newell also had arranged hotel rooms at reduced rates for these members. The trustees, the superintendent, and the residents of the home stood out in the parade procession. Everyone was said to have had a wonderful trip to San Francisco.

On May 8, 1900, in an annual report, the trustees suggested the Odd Fellows in California set up an endowment fund to support the home and its operations should national prosperity suffer. ". . .for that time is sure to come at some period, when a general financial depression throughout the country will make the burden of properly sustaining a Home heavier than the Order can afford to bear." How smart was this board! The foresight of this board of trustees for the home was always on top of things. The trustees seemed to visualize the future and take slow steps when slow steps were needed.

The year 1900 marked the first year the home report included the mortuary report. Five residents had died in this reporting period. L. N. Snyder, 68, heart failure; S. F. Lurvey, 80, fever and old age; G. Landon, 74, blood poisoning; J. F. Monhardt, 76, old age; and E. Gregory, 79, obstruction of bowels and hiccoughs. Eventually all of the deaths would be reported by name. These reports included the resident's lodge number, date of death, and birthplace.

In 1901, the home received its piano, as this was a suggestion made by the previous Grand Master a year earlier. The current Grand Master, W. W. Watson, had commented on the many aspects of the home, which he observed during his two visits. He wanted to offer in his report an impartial point of view with regard to the "perplexing questions concerning the Home that had agitated this Grand Lodge for the past few years." This statement, made in his annual report in 1901, clearly indicates there was a serious problem pertaining to the facility.

The Grand Master praised the superintendent and his wife, the matron. He was happy to see the new piano. He thought the grounds of the home were well kept. The food was good. The inmates were happy. A new hot air furnace was installed for the winter months. Concerning the light work performed by the residents, many of the inmates, as the Grand Master referred to them, simply did not want to work. The inmates were never expected to work beyond their physical capabilities, as this was only a method to keep them active, healthy, and not sedentary. Still, of the 110 inmates, many of them never left the porches or halls of the main building. The Grand Master recommended that the small amount of compensation that was paid to the inmates be stopped, as this was also a point of contention amongst the residents.

Finally, the Grand Master recommended a hospital be built at the Thermalito Home. One note: he also recommended that no smoking be allowed in some areas pertaining to the library and hallways. He was 100 years ahead of his time. The 1901 report of the trustees offered a

Grand Master William W. Watson suggested the home have a piano so the residents could be entertained (circa 1901).

similar positive report, yet included much more additional information. Grand Master Watson, after his term had ended, would eventually serve as a trustee of the home in Thermalito.

This is the back of the main building (the home). The new boiler house is to the right.

Concerning the cemetery near the facility, "Patriarchs' Rest," the trustees reported that "neat head-stones" were purchased for the graves of those who had died. The cost of each headstone was $12. There had been only four deaths during the past year.

The Endowment Fund, which was established in 1900, grew to $2,658.89, which was being kept at the German Savings & Loan Society. A large amount of this money came from the estate of R. Sargenston. Other money came from the surplus fund remaining from the Golden Jubilee of 1899.

The trustees of the home for the year included Albert F. Jones, the president of the board; J. F. Thompson, vice president; D. Newell, Daniel Flint, and John Morton.

In the 1901 annual report of the superintendent, Dr. W. M. Hilton, the names of new inmates were now being included. There had been 12 new people to move into the home during the year. The average age of all the inmates was 71 years. The report also listed those who had died during the year. Hugh Vance, 73, malarial fever; Calvin C. Stevens, 80, paralysis; William Thomas Liggett, 75, old age; Mrs. H. E. Warncke, 49, fatty degeneration of the heart. These three were laid to rest at Patriarchs' Rest in Thermalito.

Doctor Hilton asked for a new mortuary apartment for the facility. There was not a place at the home to facilitate the dead.

Finally, the last report of 1901 related to the home came from the Special Committee on Home Location. This committee had been appointed at the 1900 Annual Session of the Grand Lodge. The purpose of the committee was to locate a possible new site where a home might be established. Fifteen locations were offered in the report. Of these locations, a few stand out and are worth mentioning here: The Chadbourne place at Pleasanton, offered for a price of $35,000; the Peralta Park Hotel in San Francisco, $75,000 (including the preparation); two locations in Santa Clara, the Kennedy tract in Los Gatos and the White property at the entrance of the Alum Park Reservation. Of these mentioned sites, the committee considered the White property the most desirable.

In 1894, the lands in Santa Clara valley had been the choice of the trustees before the Thermalito property was handed free of charge to the Odd Fellows. At that time, it was only the lack of funding that had caused the trustees to choose the gift of Thermalito over Santa Clara. Seven years later, the Special Committee on Home Location rediscovered Santa Clara. This will be the precursor as to where the new home will one day be placed.

No matter what sites were considered better than the other, the Grand Lodge, the Special Committees of whatever name, the home trustees, and the Grand Masters of any given year could do nothing but wait. A year earlier, the Grand Body had resolved by vote to not close the home in Thermalito. Nor could the Grand Body gain access to the quitclaim deed until after the 5-year period. This meant no money could be derived until May of 1904. The Odd Fellows could not sell the property, as it had agreed by vote to wait 5 years to see if the "climatic conditions" had improved and the cases of malaria had been eradicated. The 5-year waiting period was only a formality. Who really thought those two conditions could ever improve? The available properties of 1901 might not be available in 1904. For now, Thermalito was home to the home. History would continue to be made at this place. People would live out their last days at this facility.

Every year, a new report was submitted. From each year to the next, these reports always seemed to have the same tone or direction. The Grand Masters distinctly liked the home or did not like the home. The reports were straightforward, as painful as some of these may have been to read or hear. The trustees presented reports maintaining a level of optimism, while the Special Committees assigned to investigate the home presented absolutely negative reports concerning the location. But the 1902 reports would have surprises.

In 1902, the Home Site Committee, along with the Grand Master and the trustees of the home, accepted a gift of a deed of property in San Jose, California, called the "White Tract." The purpose of the gifted property was to provide a "Home for Aged and Indigent Odd Fellows, their wives, widows, and orphans." However, this time, the property could be sold or disposed of in any manner seen fit by the trustees of the home. The property was a gift to the Odd Fellows from S. E. Moreland and his wife, Gertrude.

William Nicholls, Jr., was the Grand Master. On May 4, 1902, the Grand Master's second visit to the home in Thermalito during his term, he found the inmates so disturbed he recommended an Investigating Committee of three members be appointed. The inmates were concerned that their complaints to the trustees of the home fell on deaf ears. The prevailing feeling was that no one was paying attention to matters important to the residents. Another complaint was against the watchman—that he sleeps on duty. In 1902, the home had 106 inmates.

He also stated he would not report on matters relating to the climatic conditions, as the five previous Grand Masters had already made the point. He felt the subject should be dropped. The inmates were asked what they thought about a facility in San Jose. Nearly every one of the inmates expressed a desire to be in San Jose rather than Thermalito. There were only a few that would stay in Thermalito.

In his report, the Grand Master suggested a donation be made during the holiday season to a fellow member at the home, that he or she not be forgotten. (This program began in 1902 and still exists as of this writing.)

Grand Master William Nicholls, Jr. (circa 1902).

In the 1902 report submitted by the trustees of the home, the home still had in its employment Superintendent Dr. William M. Hilton and his wife, the matron. This pair had lasted longer than any others. The laundry room was lost in a fire, and a new one was built in its place; the construction took nearly 2 months. The trustees also approved the construction of a fumigating house. The residents were still performing some labor, where they earned from 5 to 15 cents a day. The trustees, in light of the San Jose property being purchased for a future home site, recommended a new hospital not be built on the Thermalito Home property, as requested a year earlier.

There were 13 deaths reported for the year: Thomas Jefferson Wood, 71, hepatitis; James Conway, 65, cancer of the stomach; Mrs. Catherine Herr, 86, old age and malaria; William Sundermeyer, 72, consumption; James Davis, 76, hepatitis; Charles Cook, 74, hemorrhage of the lungs; Earnest Dunker, 82, old age and malaria; William Quayle, 87, old age; Joseph Silva, 61, blood poisoning; Walter S. Hinman, 76, hepatitis; Oscar H. Tafts, 73, dropsy; John Westley Ashton, 69, cause unknown; Francis M. Dillian, 71, paralysis. Eight were buried in Patriarchs' Rest near the Thermalito Home.

There was no other mention of William Quayle, other than his passing and that he was a member of Camptonville Lodge No. 307. Every year that he had been a resident at the home, he had donated portions of his monthly $12 government pension to the facility. In 1846, he had been a sailor under Commodore John D. Sloat's command when Sloat took Monterey after a short and decisive sea battle. The United States claimed California after the battle.

The trustees' report included several pages on the new property in San Jose. In short, a cash prize contest was set up for the individual or architectural firm that could present the best plans for the new home site. Of course, the plans had to include the types of materials required and the estimated cost for building the structure. There could be no more than 10 competitors. First prize would be 5 per centum of the cost of the building for full plans, etc; second prize: $250; third prize: $150; fourth prize: $100. Later, the prize for first place would be changed to $300. The trustees would judge the plans. The trustees for the year were J. F. Thompson, D. Newell, D. Flint, John Morton, and A. C. Bates.

Seven sets of plans were entered in the contest. Those entering the contest were: Curtis & Wilcox, E. A. Hermann and B. J. S. Cahill of San Francisco, Wilson Wythe of Oakland, Morgan & Walls of Los Angeles, Wolfe & McKenzie, and William Binder of San Jose. The plans were numbered one through seven, without the names of the contestants.

On May 12, 1902, the trustees of the Odd Fellows home commenced to study the plans and to judge the contest. The winners would not be announced until after the Annual Sessions of the Grand Lodge.

CHAPTER 14

SAME OLD HAPPENINGS

In 1903, Grand Master Milton G. Gill stated that the plan to erect a new hospital in Thermalito, which had been approved in previous years, should not be delayed for whatever reason. There was good cause to have a hospital, even if it would be for only a short time. He asked the Grand Lodge to direct the trustees of the home to begin construction immediately. This was his only recommendation concerning the facility.

The trustees would leave the decision to build a hospital in the hands of the membership. They would ask the Grand Lodge to decide what class of hospital to build, if construction was approved.

The 1903 report of the trustees was one of the shortest to date. Of course, the same subjects were touched upon, just not in-depth. Perhaps the report was shorter because the trustees now were overseeing two projects: the home in Thermalito and the planning of a new home in San Jose. One of the trustees died suddenly during the year and that vacancy was immediately filled. J. C. Morrison was elected by the Grand Lodge's executive committee to fill the position of the late A. C. Bates.

There were also eight deaths at the home in the past year: John Yoco, 60, congestion of the brain; John Wesley Sadler, 64, cancer of the stomach; John W. Barnes, 75, malaria; Margaret Mason, 69, hepatitis; Carlos Vincent, 81, asthma and la grippe; Ellen Gibney, 67, rheumatism of the heart; Rudolph De Kruze, 76, typho-malarial fever; Andrew Garrity, 64, consumption. Six of the eight were laid to rest at Patriarchs' Rest.

Grand Master Milton G. Gill (circa 1903).

In 1903, the donor of the "White Tract" land in San Jose, S. E. Moreland, presented a petition to the Grand Lodge that basically demanded that construction of a new Odd Fellows home begin on the said property by September 1, 1903, or return the property. There had also been numerous cash donations made toward this new project, which would also have to be returned. On May 15, 1903, the Grand Body voted to begin construction in San Jose. "The calls for the ayes and noes resulted in 395 for and 224 against."

It should be noted that the per capita assessments were being increased against the lodges year after year.

The physician's report on the home in Thermalito included many of the earlier described illnesses; however, a couple of new ones did show up on the 1903 report. Cancer was now listed, as was morphine addiction, or "fiend." Malaria was still the dominant illness at the Thermalito Home. These reports offer the reader an insight as to what people suffered from and how they died.

The 1903 report was vague as there had been only a limited amount of concerns, which were documented in the year's reports. Of any year to date, this was the least reported upon. Perhaps the members were tiring of expending so much energy on the matter. But this lull would soon change.

In 1904, Grand Master C. W. Baker, after a visit to the home in Thermalito, repeated what his predecessor had stated: "The want of a hospital is very great and the Grand Lodge should direct the Trustees to proceed at once and erect the same." There were 99 men and 15 women as residents of the facility. Once again, the trustees deferred the decision of erecting a new hospital to the Grand Body.

The trustees offered some new information in its annual report, aside from the continuation of the same matters arising year after year. The residents were now given an opportunity to escape the heat of Thermalito during the summer months by taking a "short vacation" into the mountains where it was cooler. Twenty-three miles away from Thermalito, at a place called Berry Creek, the residents found refuge from the burning summer heat. It was planned that groups of eight would go to this resort area for 2-week intervals. Ironically, though the residents complained of the heat at Thermalito, there was much difficulty in finding the first eight people to go on the trip.

The trustees concluded the annual report by stating it regretted more members had never seen the home in Thermalito and praising

Grand Master Charles W. Baker (circa 1904).

the good work that had taken place, "notwithstanding the disheartening and discouraging agitation concerning the Home question that disturbs and divides the Grand Lodge each year."

By all indications, not very many members ever bothered to visit the home in Thermalito. It may have never been given a chance to prevail. As of 1904, it certainly was not given the opportunity for acceptance. The trustees saw Thermalito grow; they saw the yearly improvements; they knew it was improving, but too slowly for the membership and at a cost it was unwilling to pay. This is what the reports and records bore out year after year.

There were 10 more deaths in the reporting period: James Watson, 70, old age and scrofula; Horace Gates, 84, old age; John Forthado, 79, heart failure; Timothy Moody, 69, senile decay; William Moss, 84, old age; Alfred Himes, 75, paralysis; Emily J. McDonald, 75, old age; Frederick Hartleb, 82, old age; Douglas A. Macphee, 77, cause unknown; Charles A.Warner, 77, fatty degeneration. Seven were buried in Patriarchs' Rest.

The property in San Jose was also mentioned in great detail in the trustees' annual report. Water was the biggest concern. It seemed the "White Tract" lacked sufficient water sources, and that the wells were not adequate to support a fully functioning operation needed by a home. The trustees made the decision not to spend any more money searching for a water source.

The committee, whose job it was to find the San Jose property and its donor, rebutted. There existed several springs in the area that could be fitted with proper plumbing hardware to access the springs instead of the wells. This was one of the most detailed responses, including the method by which water would be obtained, ever listed in an Odd Fellows publication. The proposed cost of the piping project was approximately $17,000.

Was the Odd Fellows ready to accept a high price to start a new home project? Time would only tell. However, the old project would continue to expand. On May 13, 1904, the Grand Body approved the erection of a new hospital at the Thermalito.

The year 1905 marked the first year photographs of the home were included in the annual reports. Few members actually ever saw the Thermalito Home, but these images brought the truest story home and to the point. The tones of future reports gradually changed. However,

A drawing of the proposed hospital.

the pendulum was already swinging away from Thermalito as being the permanent site for the facility.

Twenty-three deaths occurred in the reporting period. This was the most deaths in a single year since the home opened in 1895. This was not going to remain the year having the most deaths. There had been 100 deaths in 10 years; 25 of those deaths happened in 1 year. Those who passed away: John Mullin, 66, anasarca; Amos Baldwin, 82, old age and paralysis; William T. Azbill, 74, old age; Fred Decker, 77, old age and paralysis; Frank H. Deidell, 75, fatty degeneration of the heart; William A. Irwin, 81, carbolic acid poisoning; Mrs. Lena Fortro, 71, carbolic acid poisoning; Louis Kaselau, 80, old age; Frank G. Guild, 80, old age; Thomas Benson, 76, malarial fever; Mary Chrismtan, 83, old age; Frederick C. Waite, 77, cause unknown; Elizabeth D. Miller, 75, old age; Horace A. Porter, 58, drowned; Francis Miller, 75, suicide by drowning in the bathtub (this would not be the last suicide at the home); Leopold Weltch, 69, Bright's disease of kidneys; Peter J. Ipsen, 81, senile gangrene; Charles A. Wikman, 51, apoplexy; John Bining, 66, rheumatism of the heart; James H. Bishop, 76, intermittent fever;

Home residents at the dining hall (circa 1907).

William A. Mason, 71, intermittent fever; John Alexander, 76, bladder cancer; Charles P. Wolcott, 77, anasarca. Nineteen were buried in Patriarchs' Rest.

Horace Porter's October 12, 1904, drowning had been witnessed by one of the residents, who was watching from a window in the facility. Mr. Ross watched Porter walk along the bank of the Feather River when Porter fell into the river. He struggled to get out of the water and actually managed to climb out of the cold water and briefly stand up when he appeared to pass out and fall backwards into the river. According to Ross, "He was swept down and out of sight in a minute or two." By the time help arrived, Porter was already submerged. Because it was late November and the water being very cold, the body would remain submerged longer. Porter's body could not be recovered until the arrival of warmer weather.

The suicide of Francis Miller was somewhat "peculiar," as it was in the *Oroville Daily Register*. It occurred the day after the accidental drowning of Horace Porter. Miller had been suffering from severe pain caused by a bad bladder. He did not want to suffer any longer. After enjoying a prepared breakfast at 7:00 a.m., Miller entered a bathroom, where he drew a tub full of water. He removed his overcoat and shoes and lay down in the water, where he drowned himself. The former 75-year-old bricklayer left behind a written message on a piece of slate, where on one side it read, "I cannot bear the pain any longer, and will not." On the other side it read, "My ills cannot be mended, but are easily ended; so here goes to turn up my toes." He definitely kept his humor to the last moment of life on this earth. There would be other unnatural deaths over the years.

The main road and the hospital. The hospital was on the east side of the home.

The hospital construction was delayed due to heavy rains that had washed out the bridge crossing the Feather River to Oroville. The home would have to wait until the rainy season passed before lumber and other supplies could be brought in from Oroville. The hospital was completed by spring of 1905.

An ice plant was needed at the home. They used enough ice to justify the construction of an ice plant. A total of 45,690 pounds of ice was purchased over the last year for $228.43. It was felt by the trustees that

Lawn area and fountain near the home's hospital.

A gathering in front of the hospital.

money could be saved should an ice plant be built on the grounds. The Grand Lodge approved the project.

The "White Tract" in San Jose was being sold for $10,000. There was no reason for the Odd Fellows to hold on to property that could not supply enough water to support a home. The search for new sites would continue. But a new site would not be found for another 3 years, after much debate. The year 1905 was in the books and would soon become another forgotten year.

On April 18, 1906, tragedy struck the Independent Order of Odd Fellows in California. The great earthquake and fire struck San Francisco, destroying the office of the Grand Lodge. Dozens of lodges were displaced in the city. Members died. Members were left with nothing. Members and their families were homeless. Attention seemed to be given to the situation at hand, and not as much to the home in distant Thermalito.

Grand Master John W. Linscott (circa 1905).

The Grand Master still found time to include a short report. Grand Master W. W. Phelps followed the last year's report made by Past Grand Master John W. Linscott, where he agreed, "It is a burning shame and disgrace to the great Order of Odd Fellows in California, that the Grand Lodge should permit a single one of our wards to be compelled to sleep in such a place." He was referring to residents having to sleep in the crowded, hot, third-story attic due to lack of space. He was not happy with Thermalito.

He wanted to see the Odd Fellows purchase a new site for the home. Period. He did not want to settle for locations just because they were gifts, stating, "...we should go into the market and purchase what we want." That was all he had alluded to in his report. Grand Master Phelps had once served on the Special Committee on the I.O.O.F. Home, which investigated the home years earlier. His suggestion to relocate could not have been a surprise.

The trustees of the home reported the construction of an ice plant was completed. The Cyclops Iron Works constructed the ice machine and its motor. The cost was $800. The machine produced 600 pounds of ice, which was a welcomed gift to the inmates who endured the hot, dry, summer days. The electric bill to run the ice machine and the new refrigerator unit was $3, but worth every cent.

The trustees commented on the success of having photographs included with the 1905 report of the home. Every member could witness the good works being performed by the Odd Fellows. (Because it was so successful, photographs would be printed in all future reports for the next several years.)

On a sad note, the superintendent and his wife, the matron, resigned their employment and left on January 1, 1906. Dr. and Mrs. Hilton had been at the facility for about 5 years. The trustees tried in vain to keep them at the home. Thus, there was no report made concerning who was ill for the year. The list of those who died lacked the cause of death, and no longer was the final resting place mentioned.

A beautiful new hospital was constructed as well, where chronically ill patients were transferred into the hospital. Residents who had been in the attic were placed into the rooms of those who were moved to the hospital.

In 1906, Grand Master William W. Phelps had greater concerns than the home, as the 1906 earthquake and fire destroyed the Grand Lodge in San Francisco. He would focus his attention on saving the Order and ensuring a convention would be held for the year.

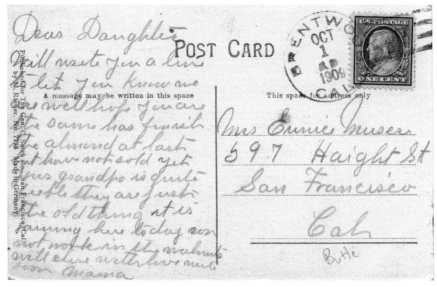

The original hospital before it burned down in 1908. A new one would be rebuilt in its place within a year.

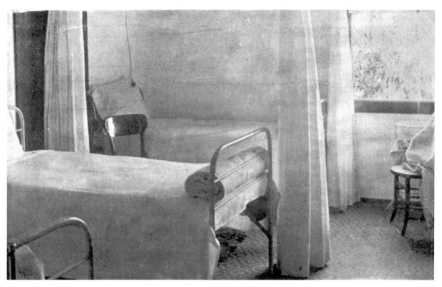

A typical room at the hospital.

More deaths occurred in this period than in any other in the history of the Thermalito Home. Twenty-seven died. (A complete list is included in the last chapter of this book.)

In San Jose, the "White Tract" was sold for $13,000 to Charles C. Benson. That episodic adventure of locating a new home site was ended; another was soon to come. There still existed a Special Committee appointed to search for a new site.

The trustees for the term included: John Morton, John Thompson, W. W. Watson, H. E. Howard, and S. E. Moreland. (Moreland was the member who had donated the San Jose property to the Odd Fellows 3 years earlier.) He was the second donor to have served on the home board.

The next term brought Theodore A. Bell, a Grand Master who saw the home for all of the good things that had been attained by the Order. For him, the presence of a home for the older and needy members of the Order and the hard work being done to make their last days peaceful was enough. It was an honorable testament to the Odd Fellows of California. He also praised the superintendent, T. W. Prose, and his wife,

Grand Master Theodore A. Bell. He found little to fault in the
home's operations (circa 1907).

the matron. In 1907, he offered no complaints or conditions as his
predecessors had for many years. He actually reported, in-depth, on his
visit to the Orphans Home in Gilroy, where he praised the Rebekahs for
their good work.

By 1907, the home in Thermalito had welcomed 320 elderly
people. The number accepted in 1907 alone was 130, the most since its
opening in 1895. The property was valued at $100,000. At this point,
this was one of the most active homes in the Order. Although the
Sovereign Grand Lodge prohibited the construction of a home
through assessments of lodges and membership, it did permit the
assessments of lodges to fund the operation of a home. And this is how
California found the money to continue having a home. The Odd
Fellows definitely had its home!

The home's trustees hard at work. This meeting took place on the porch of the hospital (circa 1906).

In addition to the inmates, the home was now employing an engineer, a superintendent, a matron, a caretaker, a person to work the commissary, a man to do odd jobs (a choreman), a dishwasher, dairyman, farmer, fireman, watchman, porter, laundryman, nurses, chambermaids, cooks, waiters, and extra laborers. The home also hired office workers, attorneys, and others when needed. The trustees oversaw the entire operations.

Meanwhile, as reported by the trustees, improvements were always being done at the Thermalito Home. Someone unfamiliar with the history of the facility or the sentiment of many members of the Order must have thought the Odd Fellow home was never going to leave Thermalito.

On a positive note, one of the inmates sewed a new flag for the home. "We feel it to be our duty to call the attention of the Grand Lodge, the splendid and skillful work of Sister Wilcox in making for the Home a new flag." Handmade flags must have been beautiful; this is an art rarely found today.

CONDITIONS OF PROPOSAL OF SITE FOR
ODD FELLOWS' NEW HOME.

Circular Letter No. 1.

SAN FRANCISCO, August 10, 1906.

At the session of the Grand Lodge, I. O. O. F., of the State of
California, held at Santa Cruz, California, during the month of June
1906, the undersigned were appointed by the Grand Lodge, a Special
Committee to select and purchase a site for an Odd Fellows Home,
subject to the approval of the Standing Committee of such Grand
Lodge.

On the tenth day of August, 1906, the Committee met at the office
of the Trustees of the Odd Fellows Home, at 458 Duboce Avenue,
San Francisco, California, and duly organized by electing John Morton,
President, and W. W. Watson, Secretary.

Pursuant to the duties and powers vested in the Committee, we
hereby invite offers of sites, suitable for the purposes of an Odd
Fellows Home, which offers must comply substantially with the following conditions, to-wit: The site to contain not less than forty
(40), nor more than one hundred and twenty (120) acres, and must
be good tillable land, well watered, and within three hours travel of
San Francisco; and full and complete answers to the following questions must accompany each offer, to-wit:

1. How many acres in tract?.....

2. Briefly describe nature and character of the soil.....

3. Is the land rolling, level or hilly?.....

4. What is the elevation?.....

5. What native trees or crops now on the land?.....

6. Number of acres tillable....., and number of acres
under cultivation?.....

7. Where is land located?.....
....., and
how approached .....
and time and means of transportation.....
and distance from San Francisco.....

8. What improvements, if any?.....

9. What is the source, nature and capacity of the water supply,
at the present time?.....

10. Is it capable of further development, and if so, how?.....

11. What are the facilities for drainage and the disposition of
sewage? .....

12. Are there any especial building sites on the tract,.....
and if so, state character of same.....

13. Distance to nearest town and postoffice.....

14. Are there any saloons in the vicinity of the tract, where liquor
can be obtained?.....
And if so, distance therefrom?.....

15. State the lowest net cash price.....

The questions for the trustees to answer when searching for
grounds for a new home site (circa 1906).

More deaths. Sixteen deaths occurred in this reporting period; the trustees resumed the practice of listing not only the names of each, but also the ages and causes of death. But the reports no longer indicate where the departed were laid to rest. Those who departed: John MacFarlane, 87, gastritis and senility; Mathew Jansen, 83, chronic bronchitis; George W. Herron, 76, consumption; Hans Peter Nelson, 59, septicaemia; George W. Richison, 77, gastroenteritis; Adam Volk, 72, valvular disease of the heart; Mrs. Jane Millner, 75, acute peritonitis; John Peter Baette, 76, gastritis; William Becker, 89, senility; Riley Singletary, 78, pneumonia; Matthew Fleming, 64, consumption; John Jacob Wagner, 75, chronic bronchitis; W. C. Wilkerson, 80, enterocolitis; Harvey Turner, 81, senility; Mrs. Susan Dains, 74, cerebral hemorrhage; and J. S. Barner, 79, basilar meningitis. In 1907, the reports by name of those who fell ill during the year were also resumed.

The Special Committee assigned to locate a new site for the home was virtually stopped in its tracks because of the disruption by the 1906

The trustees in 1907.

earthquake and fire. The Grand Lodge office had been destroyed. However, the committee met long enough to draw up a questionnaire to send to several real estate agents in the San Francisco area. There were 67 sites brought to the attention of this committee! The committee physically inspected nearly all those submitted sites. It was determined to find a new location for the Odd Fellows home. Was Thermalito really that despised? Was this eagerness the result a nonacceptance of the assessments on the lodges? Or was it truly because Thermalito was a terrible place to have a home? Those questions were most likely answered years earlier.

The Special Committee could not afford to make a mistake when it came to locating the new spot for the home. It summed it up by stating, "We had better move slowly and be sure."

CHAPTER 15

THE BEGINNING OF THE END FOR THE THERMALITO HOME

An artful poster representing the Odd Fellows Home in Thermalito.

Grand Master F. B. Ogden reported in 1908 that the Site Committee located an acceptable place to build a new home. After examining 80 different properties in less than 2 years, the committee selected an 85-acre site with 5,000 fruit trees close to Saratoga Springs in Santa Clara County. The name of this site was Oakwood Farm. It had enough water, meeting the major requirement set by the Grand Body 2 years earlier. The cost of the property was $16,000, which was approved by a special meeting held on February 24, 1908. This site as described was well-researched, and no doubt met the political wants and needs of many in the Order. Shortly thereafter, on March 20, 1908, the Odd Fellows purchased the Oakwood Farm from John W. Stetson and Bessie Harden Stetson.

The Thermalito Home had been operating for 12 years and improved each and every year. It had the main house, with additional housing for over 130 inmates. There were well-maintained barns, an ice house, blacksmith shop, a cottage, a house for the superintendent and his wife, a new hospital, and numerous other structures used for the everyday operation of the home. There was a small mortuary and a cemetery where many of those who died now rest. Thermalito was nearly self-sufficient. It had become a small city. No doubt the expansion of the home aided in the building of the town itself. (Until the home was established and before citizens were hired to work there, little, if anything, stood in the "Thermalito Colony." The property was to be a resort and that deal had fallen through, costing the developers their dream as well as additional wealth. They ended up giving the hotel to the Odd Fellows. Now, after 12 years, the end to a struggle was coming.)

Concerning the location of the home in Thermalito, the Grand Master reported there was not a single negative comment. His report was quite the opposite from any of his predecessors who had never praised the home. In response to the site just purchased in Santa Clara County, he stated, "I hope and trust we have made no mistake in this step. It means a loss of many thousands of dollars to make the change . . ." This passage, by Grand Master Ogden, seemed to indicate the home had finally met its goal of being a respectable Odd Fellow Home for

Grand Master Frank B. Ogden (circa 1908).

The Aged and Infirmed. Despite all that had been accomplished, however, the home would not remain in Thermalito. It was too late. A new
site had already been located for a new facility.

Twenty-five residents had passed away during the reporting year
of 1908. The trustees reported the following names, ages, and causes;
however, they, once again, declined to make mention of where these
people had been laid to rest: Joshua Webb, 80, acute pleuritis; Tamma

A 1910 photo of the cow barns and woodshed.

Hurd, 75, cerebral hemorrhage; Joseph Burdick, 74, heart disease; Epenetus Wallace, 84, softening of the brain; William Roberts, 75, softening of the brain; James E. Payton, 77, paralysis; A. P. Christensen, 81, angina pectoris; W. L. McKay, 77, cerebral thrombosis; Asa B. Jenny, 65, suicide; Ann Startin, 65, chronic gastritis; G. W. Williamson, 74, heart disease; Gustave Eymat, 66, accidentally killed by electric car; Francis W. Peabody, 77, heart failure; John H. Mitchell, 86, senility; D. D. Green, 85, senility; Amos J. Ross, 78, rheumatism; Sumner McCausland, 75, chronic bronchitis; Louis H. Nolte, 82, chronic bronchitis; Chauncey Langdon, 80, hemorrhage of the brain; Thomas W. Edwards, 72, pericarditis; F. C. Hahn, 78, bronchitis; George W. Carswell, 80, pneumonia; Rix A. Johnston, 73, pneumonia; Andrew F. Brown, 72, pneumonia; August Bansch, 78, valvular lesion of the heart.

In the case of Gustave Eymat's accidental death, he had been hit by a Chico-bound Northern Electric car on November 22, 1907. The accident happened about six o'clock in the evening. He was unconscious and still clinging to life at midnight. His skull had been fractured and his left leg broken. No one knew his identity at the time

Sister Bowman and Brother Becker, the oldest residents in the home (circa 1906).

of the incident, so he was taken to the Sister's Hospital in Chico, where doctors gave "no hope of his recovery." The *Daily Oroville Register* reported, "While in a half-conscious condition he murmured over and over some name that sounded very much as if it might be 'Don.'" Eymat died on November 24, 1907. It was not until the next day, after his death, that he was identified by Dr. T. W. Prose of the Odd Fellows home. Eymat was a Frenchman, also a member of the Franco American Lodge #207 of San Francisco. He had been a resident of the home for only a month before his fatal accident.

On October 23, 1907, Asa B. Jenny committed suicide. Jenny was suffering from paralysis for a year. When doctors had informed him there would be no hope of recovery, he replied, "there is no good reason why I should live longer." The 65-year-old cut his throat with a razor. He was found dead lying on his bed with the razor on the floor. He had no relatives. Jenny's suicide would not be the last suicide at the home, as others would choose a similar ending over the agony of long-spelled suffering.

A mining company, represented by Charles Helman, leased the bottom land property (a part of the Thermalito property sitting immediately adjacent to the Feather River), for the purpose of dredging. This was the popular method used in the area for mining gold. The trustees leased the land for $22,000 for a period of 10 years, a considerable sum of money in 1908.

A 65,000-gallon reservoir was constructed to supply water in case of fire and for domestic use. Water was fed to the home by a newly built plumbing system. A roof was built over the reservoir. The telephone company installed a more efficient telephone system. Additional woodsheds were constructed for the hospital and the laundry room. Improvements and maintenance never slowed down at the Thermalito site.

The trustees for this term were John Morton, W. W. Watson, John Thompson, H. C. Howard, and S. E. Moreland, 1908. They had little to say in the way of any recommendations related to the new home site, saying ". . .the Grand Lodge itself is the best judge as to any action concerning the new site."

A 1909 photograph of the covered reservoir. The Commissary Department is to the right.

In 1909, Grand Master John E. Raker stated his pleasure with the home operation in Thermalito. The facility's doctor, Dr. T. W. Prose, especially impressed him; his care toward the residents was exceptional.

On November 25, 1908, the hospital at the home in Thermalito was burned to the ground. It was a misfortune. Since there was already an overtaxed amount of space inside the facility, it was nearly impossible to place those who had been in the hospital in the wings of the home. It was regrettable, but one member perished in the fire. His name was John B. Thompson (no relation to the presiding home trustee). He ignored the pleas to stay out of the burning building. The superintendent reported Mr. Thompson "was a little demented and it is supposed that he did not realize his danger when he returned to the building." There would have been more deaths, but the superintendent worked fast to get everyone out of the hospital.

The month prior to the hospital burning, there had been an explosion of a hot-water heater in the kitchen. The night watchman was blamed due to his miscommunication with another watchman. He

On January 1, 1906, Dr. T. W. Prose and his wife were hired as superintendent and matron.

Grand Master John E. Raker (circa 1909).

forgot to tell his replacement not to light the fire to the heater, as there had been some earlier trouble with a leaking hot-water pipe. Nobody was injured, and this also caused needed and desired improvements to be made to the kitchen.

Plans to rebuild the hospital were set into motion immediately. In the meantime, the displaced inmates of the hospital were set up in the sewing room, library, hallways, and any other places that could be used as bed space. A "bungalow" was nearing completion, which would eventually become the new residence for many of the displaced inmates.

A picture of the new hospital in 1910. It was rebuilt after a fire destroyed the previous hospital just months earlier.

A side view of the home's second hospital in 1910.

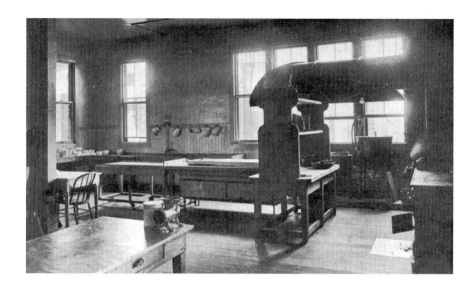

Two views of the kitchen as seen in 1909. This must have been unbearably hot in the summertime.

The "Bungalow" in 1909. The photo on the above left is the front of the bungalow. The photo on the above right depicts the home's team of horses and surrey in front of the bun-

It should be pointed out the Grand Master questioned the need of having Life Memberships at the home. This had been the practice since the inception of the facility. Residents always had an option to purchase a Life Membership there; this had not been a concern to any previous Grand Master until now. The Grand Master said, "Some of those with

Residents enjoy a ride around the home's grounds (circa 1905).

Life Memberships feel they have more liberty and more rights than the regular residents of the Home." In actuality, holding membership in any capacity, opting to pay membership dues annually, or to pay one time for a lifetime did not give a member an advantage or increase his status as an Odd Fellow. All members had equal status.

An envelope mailed by resident Edward Price to his wife in 1904. Price passed away February 9, 1909.

The trustees in 1909.

Residents were permitted to go to Oroville Tuesdays and Fridays. Some attended Odd Fellows meetings while others socialized with local citizens. A team of horses would take them to town if they wished to go on these designated days. Oroville was the closest town, located just across the Feather River unless, of course, one looks at the Thermalito Home as being a "small town."

Seventeen residents died in the reporting period from May of 1908 to May of 1909. The trustees reported the following names: J. Oscar Tainter, 83, senile bronchitis; Richard Pryor, 65, septicaemia; Thomas Jarvis, 72, heart disease; Robert Bandurant, 81, senility; J. H. Page, 78, senility; Charles Schroeder, 85, enterocolitis; Azuba E. Freeman, 79, stomach trouble; Isaac E. Baker, 80, senility; Ole Tobias, 78, enterocolitis; J. B. Thompson, 57, burned to death; Cornelius Reynolds, 82, cerebral hemorrhage; A. W. Eskridge, 77, chronic cystitis; Mary E. Price, 73, chronic gastritis; H. C. Baker, 79, paralysis; Morris Marks, 73, softening of the brain; Edward Price, 72, senility; S. A. Laine, 79, gastric hemorrhage.

All other business at the home was normal. Donations were still being made to it. The crops were doing fantastic. There were no cases of malaria reported by the physician. Inmates were still volunteering to work when needed. There was still no firm decision to build in Santa

Grand Master Grove L. Johnson (circa 1910).

Clara valley, the future home site; nevertheless, the Grand Lodge directed the Site Committee to have plans prepared to erect a new home by the next year's annual session. The lodges would also be assessed a per capita of 30 cents per member for the year, which would be used for the new facility. There were no complaints made on record as there had been when the home was established in Thermalito 14 years earlier.

The trustees for this past term included the following: John Thompson, H. C. Howard, S. E. Moreland, D. A. Sinclair, and John

Unity Cottage in 1910.

The back view and yard of Unity Cottage.

Hazlet. Hazlet replaced John Morton, who resigned after serving 9 years on the board.

Grove L. Johnson, the Grand Master reporting in 1910 on the home in Thermalito, offered the shortest report of all his predecessors. It was only eight sentences long. Aside from praising the good work being accomplished there, he did recommend a brick or concrete foundation be placed under the bungalow, inferring it had no proper foundation:

> "I visited the Home at Thermalito and carefully examined the same. It is in very good condition, but needs some changes. I recommend that the hospital be remodeled so as to remove the kitchen and dining room from the center of the building. At present they are dependent upon a skylight for air and artificial light at all hours. I recommend that the bungalow be raised and a brick or concrete foundation be placed underneath. I recommend that the side moulding in the bedrooms of the main building be removed and iron bedsteads be installed in lieu of the wooden ones now in use. The grounds are well kept and furnish occupation and pleasure to the inmates. Dr. Burgess and his wife, the superintendent and matron, are deserving of commendation for the manner in which they have conducted the affairs of the Home."

In the report by the trustees of the home, it was reported that the expenditures made there were the most of any other year. There were some causes for this drastic increase of spending. The hospital was rebuilt; there were more residents; the cost of living increased; and the Unity Cottage was constructed to make room for additional residents. There had not been an increase in per capita assessments for a long while, only the 10-cent increase requested in 1909. A sum of $6,800 was used to build the new two-story Unity Cottage. According to the trustees, this was the best building on the property.

Superintendent T. W. Prose and his wife, the matron, resigned early in the year. They were replaced by George Waldo Burgess and his wife (the matron), who would remain in these positions until June 1, 1916.

As had been the case for many years, various societies of Oroville continued to make visits to the home, interacting with the residents. On Sundays, everyone was encouraged to attend religious services in Oroville. Sometimes the Rebekahs from Oroville entertained the "old people," as they were also called. Members of lodges throughout the state had come en mass to visit the residents. The Sacramento Odd Fellows Relief Committee came to visit too. On June 14, 1909, even the "Grand Master of Masons of California," along with his Grand Officers, stopped by to pay their respects.

There was a lot of traffic in and out of the home property. There were annual Fourth of July celebrations on the grounds that brought people from all over the region. The St. Elmo Company had performed at the home as well. The home was in some respect a small social center in which many outsiders came to enjoy themselves and make life a little more interesting for those residents needing the interaction.

The New Home Farm in Santa Clara County was supplying the Thermalito Home with dried fruits that had been grown and processed on the property. The Odd Fellows did not sit and wait for a new home to be constructed but sought to make this new acquisition pay for itself. Not only was the Thermalito Home being supplied with dried fruits, such as apples, peaches, plums, apricots, pears, and lots of prunes, it was making a profit from selling fresh fruit on the market as well.

According to all of the reports, water and the supplying of water was the greatest concern to the new home site. However, this goal was eventually met by the digging of wells and establishing a network of pipes. There were few obstacles remaining for the move from Thermalito to the Oakwood Farm.

Once again, as in previously years, the Grand Lodge and the Board of Odd Fellows Home Trustees decided to hold a contest, where prize money would be awarded to the top plans for construction of a new home on the Santa Clara County property (Oakwood Farm) near Saratoga. First prize would be $400 cash; second place, $250; and third place, $150. There were many specifications the Odd Fellows had made with regard to the planning of the new facility.

The trustees of the home in front of Unity Cottage in 1910.

Reports began citing the new property as being "near Saratoga." Eventually, encroachment and growth of the surrounding community would envelope the Oakwood Farm. Oakwood would be located in "Saratoga" per se. On April 8, 1910, the Grand Lodge ended up with eight sets of plans for the new home. First place "was awarded to J. M. Boehrer and R. W. Hart of San Francisco, the second prize to Cummins & Weymouth of Oakland, the third prize to Wolfe & McKenzie of San Jose."

Twenty-five residents died in this reporting period. Samuel Crady Edwards, 82, heart disease; Charles Frank Laramie, 79, heart failure; Gustav Leuders, 66, rheumatism affecting the heart; Henry Horton, 83, acute gastritis; Franz Schmauss, 85, diabetes; Hugh Montgomery, 71, pulmonary tuberculosis; Ed Hopes, 73, valvular disease; Cornelius N. Gray, 89, gastroenteritis; S. B. Jarnigan, 73, uremia complicating chronic Bright's disease; Thomas Rutter, 76, cancer of the neck and throat; George B. Densmore, 82, mental debility and senility; Mrs. Eunice Briggs, 91, senility; Isaac Washington Barber, 72, no cause

Grand Master Thomas W. Duckworth (circa 1911).

listed; J. D. Spencer, 79, senility; William J. Nicholson, 87, chronic Bright's disease; Henry Provost, 69, no cause listed; John Kean, 76, apoplexy; E. J. McCourtney, 87, general paralysis and senility; Mrs. Antoinette Burdick, 76, killed in railway accident; Peter Devault, 76, senility and general debility; James McGranahan, 84, congestion of the lungs; Hermann Hake, 81, senile gangrene complicating valvular disease of the heart; Charles Wentworth, 85, pleuropneumonia; E. D. Burger, 83, hemorrhage of the lungs; and John Patterson, 84, pulmonary tuberculosis, age, and debility.

On April 9, 1910, Unity Cottage was dedicated by Past Grand Master William H. Barnes. This is important in that the Thermalito Home was still officially expanding. The Odd Fellows continued investing money into this home site even thought they did not intend to maintain the facility at this location. The fact the Odd Fellows were even taking the time to dedicate the new structures at a location it would vacate in just 2 more years is surprising.

Again, it is ironic the Odd Fellows had a fully operating home at Thermalito with all the consideration and attention made over a 15-year period, and yet, sought to build another home. Perhaps having two homes for the aged and infirmed might have been considered. Abandoning Thermalito would seem a waste of years and investment. The consideration for the aforementioned was never mentioned in the reports. Keep in mind there were other jurisdictions with multiple homes. Pennsylvania had eight of them.

The home trustees for the term were John Thompson, S. E. Moreland, D. A. Sinclair, John Hazlett, and Fred E. Pierce.

With regard to his visit with the residents of the home, Grand Master T. W. Duckworth said the following: "They appeared to be as well-contented as one could expect; old, tired, worn out brothers and sisters to be." He also praised the superintendent and the matron. Nothing else was said by the Grand Master.

In 1911, the home trustees learned from the State Board of Health it was the mosquitoes that caused malaria at the facility. Now, the goal was to eradicate the mosquitoes.

There had been a small post office set up at the home. The superintendents that were employed throughout the years were also postmasters, but this particular activity was now deemed unwarranted because of the time spent picking up the mail from the station. Instead, the trustees were hopeful a new station would soon be established near the home.

A graphophone had been acquired during the year and new records were purchased for the residents to enjoy themselves. There were still numerous donations being made to the home, everything from cash to books and cigars.

The annual reports of the trustees were becoming shorter since the Santa Clara County property near Saratoga was purchased. There was no longer anything concerning the home about which to argue. A new home would be constructed on a site acceptable to the majority—period. The trustees no longer defended the original facility in Thermalito. The previous years' complaints by those opposed to Thermalito were no longer needed. Those who opposed the home in Thermalito had won.

According to the 1911 report, the trustees reported 23 residents died during the year. However, as done a few years earlier, the report declined to state where those who had died were buried. Those who died: George W. Andrews, 64, pulmonary tuberculosis; Joseph Libby Bangs, 76, chronic nephritis and cystitis; B. B. Jackson, 96, senility; E. Warneke, 69, paraplegia, hematuria with uremia; John A. Holm, 70, Bright's disease, valvular disease of the heart, hematemesis; J. G. Dickinson, 74, pulmonary tuberculosis; Samuel G. McPherson, 82, uremia; Corder David Glenn, 80, carbuncle disease of the stomach, inanition; Mrs. Roseanna Bauman, 90, cardiac asthma, senility; James J. Warner, 57, apoplexy, acute gastritis; Mrs. A. Stratton, 73, senility and general debility; William B. Kimball, 53, meningitis; Mrs. Sarah E. Morris, 74, cancer of uterus and adnexa; James W. Archibald, 78, valvular disease of the heart; Mrs. Jane M. Reed, 57, valvular disease of the heart, cerebral embolism; Joshua Albright, 81, acute gastritis; John Foster, 84, valvular disease of the heart, nephritis pneumonia; Mrs. Anna Wuthrich, 61, cerebral hemorrhage; John Kimberlin, 74, cerebral hemorrhage; Dan Sutherland, 83, congestion of the lungs, senility; Hugh Walker, 68, Bright's disease; James McCurry, 79, Bright's disease with dropsy; and William D. Young, 81, no cause reported.

By 1911, Patriarchs' Rest, the cemetery at Thermalito, was significantly being occupied by each year's deaths. These departed Odd Fellows had lived and died at the home. They had been part of the small community which had grown from one central building into a near township. What would happen to the cemetery when the home moved from Thermalito? This was to be questioned, but it never became a great concern.

Front View of Administration Building, Odd Fellows Home, California

The new home in Saratoga in 1912.

Oroville, Cal.
Home of the I. O. O. F.

This postcard was mailed in the month of August, 1912. Obviously, the writer has a sense of humor, writing that it is "nice and cool here."

Another view of the Odd Fellows home. Note: the early automobile in front of the home.

Meanwhile, at the "New Home Site" near Saratoga, the grounds were being prepared. Trees were planted. Electrical poles were erected and electrical lines installed on the grounds. Saratoga resident Mr. C. A. Johnson was contracted to keep trees on the property trimmed. He kept the wood, while paying the Odd Fellows $120. Wells were dug and the supply of water was considered "inexhaustible" by the trustees. By April 1, 1911, the bids for the new structure had been submitted. There were several bids considered. The trustees looked at the individual bids per each detailed task, but considered the lowest bid of contractor Henry Jacks as a whole. Henry Jacks' bid to construct the new facility near Saratoga was $182,600. Including the other bids for additional needs of the building project, the total price to build the new home would be $224,243.45. The price would eventually increase as all aspects of the construction were not included. This caused a change to the way the trustees would handle the bids. In addition to the bids, a drawing of the future home was provided to the board as well. Later, it was decided to break the jobs and bids down to individual contractors. This would save some money and allow bids to come in for each phase of the construction project. The decision of whose bids were to be accepted would be reported by the trustees in 1912.

At the close of 1911, the trustees, John Thompson, S. E. Moreland, D. A. Sinclair, John Hazlett, and Fred E. Pierce, were the same members who made up the board during the previous year. This was one of the few times a new trustee had not joined the board. Most likely it was due to there being a need of having experienced board members who understood all of the aspects of both home sites: the one in full operation and that one to be constructed. Besides, which board had the most experience in dealing with harsh criticisms for the past 16 years or so? It knew how to handle difficult people and would be able to stand up to those with complaints or concerns. The pending transition from Thermalito would not be a simple task and required the most knowledgeable members.

The trustees were directed to begin building immediately, as soon as funding became available. The Grand Master and Grand Secretary were given authorization on behalf of the Grand Lodge to borrow "a sum not exceeding One Hundred and Fifty Thousand Dollars" for the completion of the new home. Things were moving quickly now. On May 15, 1912, the Grand Lodge, by resolution, was directed to sell or lease the properties in Thermalito.

CHAPTER 16

THE TRANSITION BEGINS

The year 1912 marked the transition year for the Odd Fellows home. Thermalito was on its way out as far as everyone was concerned. The trustees of the home wanted in any way possible to maintain the facility in Thermalito. Never once was there mention of the Order needing to find another location for the home in the reports. The trustees never approached the subject. However, the majority, who were made up of members who never even saw the Thermalito Home, demanded the home be elsewhere—anywhere but Thermalito.

Once the Grand Lodge had acquired the necessary money for building the new home in Saratoga, the trustees were compelled to begin construction. It was the Odd Fellows lodges and individual members who funded the project by purchasing the Certificates of Indebtedness. These were certificates, also called "Six Per Cent New Home Notes." The Grand Lodge guaranteed payment of 6 percent per annum. An amount of $159,300 was raised through the selling of the certificates. There were lodges that invested large sums of money (considered large in that time period) in the new home. The idea of offering a 6 percent return and making this an investment was an incredibly smart move on the Grand Lodge's part. The Thermalito Home never received this kind of initial funding. Cash donations had been made to the Thermalito Home and arrived in much smaller amounts.

Concordia Lodge No. 122 invested the most money: $10,000. Of the many members who invested, W. W. Young, Charles Trautner, Walter A. Bonynge, Charles and Jesse Dick, and William Sandrock each invested $5,000. Again, this was a lot of money in 1912.

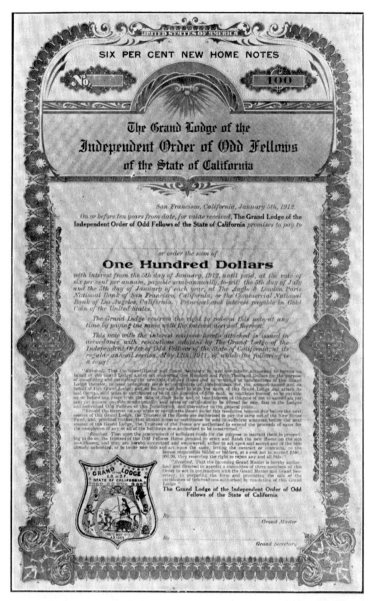

Form of Six Per Cent New Home Notes

The Grand Lodge sold notes, called "Six Per Cent New Home Notes," just like this one, to finance the new home in Saratoga. These were sold to anyone who was willing to purchase them, for a 6 percent profit.

Grand Master George F. Hudson (circa 1912). He presided at the cornerstone ceremony at the new Saratoga facility.

On October 7, 1911, the cornerstone was laid for the home. Many speeches were delivered at this grand affair. Dignitaries came from all over the state. The trustees of the home were congratulated for their work in putting together much of this new project. William H. Barnes, one of the original trustees of the home board (two had passed away), spoke of the harsh criticisms in which the trustees had to endure from the membership. He spoke of how the trustees quelled those criticisms and met all of the challenges head-on. He stated, "And our Brother Trustees of the Old Board saw that golden hour for the Thermalito Home ere they passed away. But, demands not to be ignored came for

Grand Master Hudson and home trustees in 1912 at the cornerstone ceremony.

a larger and more extensive building and grounds and Committees were directed to provide the same. Immediately came the queries 'How can you get the money?' 'Where is the security?' and similar pessimistic ejaculations, but promised faith of the Odd Fellows of California is an asset better than any banking institution." The new home had been established.

The trustees offered its report for 1912. The board had nothing out of the ordinary to report, although the home did receive some honored visitors during the year. James Harris, the Grand Treasurer of the Grand Lodge, visited the Thermalito Home. The trustees of the Grand Lodge visited as well. In addition, Judge William D. Wells, president of the board of trustees of the Masonic Home, and Mr. Hartman, the superintendent of the Masonic Home, came for a 2-day visit. Others from the Masonic Order visited too. Even the Grand Master for the Masons visited later in the year. Perhaps the Masons were scouting the site for its own future purposes. Or, maybe the Odd Fellows invited these dignitaries to visit the site in hopes of not wasting a ready-made home that would need to be sold. One could only surmise the reasons behind these visits, especially when another new Odd Fellows home was being constructed.

Again, other than the visitations from many special guests, nothing new occurred at the Thermalito Home. There were 23 deaths to report: Mrs. H. L. Carswell, 72, uremia; Charles Bowman, 73, tuberculosis; J. W. Hill, 75, senile dementia; Papstista Papa, 72, senility and debility; Mrs. E. F. McGowen, 78, internal hemorrhage, cancer of the stomach; P. H. McIntosh, 79, senility and debility, heat prostration; W. C. Bates, 77, senile dementia; A. I. Ross, 85, gastric hemorrhage, acute gastroenteritis; F. F. Galeria, 58, cancer of the stomach and liver; Mrs. B. Hahn, 80, suicide; Mrs. M. Walton, 85, endocarditic cholelithiasis; S. J. Filer, 79, valvular disease of the heart, senility, general debility; W. D. Saffory, 81, cirrohsis of liver, chronic rheumatism; M. Parker, 78, hemorrhage of the lungs, pulmonary tuberculosis; Mrs. E. Hart, 83, cancer of the stomach, senility, general debility; M. M. O'Brien, 74, cancer of the bladder, obstruction at end of the stomach; Mrs. E. Dugan, 75, congestion of the lungs, senile dementia; E. Biggs, 85, cerebral hemorrhage, locomotor ataxia, senility; Mrs. M. J. Bradley, 78, chronic nephritis, epilepsy; Mrs. M. Tufts, 94, cancer of the stomach, senility, and debility; William R. Knight, 82, suicide; W. B. Overton, 54, gastroenteritis; and Michael Finney, 81, senile dementia. The home had seen two suicides during the year where there had been no more than one in any prior given year. Also, the diagnosis of dementia was new; before 1911, the term was not used.

On September 14, 1911, at 3:00 in the morning, Mrs. B. Hahn calmly walked out of the home to the fish pond. She lay down in the water, which was only a foot deep, and drowned herself. The *Oroville Mercury* newspaper reported that "she lay prone on her back until the end arrived." After an alarm was sounded at 3:05 a.m., she was discovered within 15 minutes. She was wearing only a night garment. It was said she suffered from severe pain and "had been of morose mind for several months."

After 16 years of living at the home, William R. Knight ended his life by slashing his throat with a razor. On the morning of January 24, 1912, he was not present at the breakfast roll-call. Dr. Burgess went to

On September 14, 1911, resident Mrs. Hahn drowned herself in this pond in front of the home. The water was only a foot deep (this photo was taken in 1907).

find Knight. It was too late. Knight was taking his last dying gasps when the doctor discovered him lying on a bed with his throat cut and a bloody razor in his right hand. Knight had been a member of Mariposa Lodge #39 for over 50 years. There would be no more suicides ever again at the home.

The trustees of the home had overseen the new home project in Saratoga. One of the most important tasks involved in erecting the new facility was the determination of whose bids would be accepted. The review of bids was an ongoing job for the trustees as they had broken down all phases of the project into various levels of construction. Rather than hire one general contractor to conduct the entire job, it was less expensive to bid out each stage of construction. Here is a breakdown of the responsibilities and the bids accepted by the trustees:

Hart & Boehrer, architects ($10,000)
Henry Cowell Lime & Cement Co. ($11,250)
Z. O. Field, cement contract ($61,142)
William Bros & Henderson, finishing contract ($119,000)
San Jose Transfer Co., drayage ($750)
Robert W. Hunt & Co., testing cement ($200)
H. D. Grayson, superintendent of construction ($1,500)
J. C. Hurley, heating and water equipment ($17,904)
Maxwell Hardware Co., hardware contract ($1,494.36)
Thomas Day Co., gas fixtures ($1,900)
Various small contracts ($1,200)
Contracts estimated ($10,000)
Total: $236,342.36

This was below the amount of $240,000 the Grand Lodge had authorized the trustees to use. By the end of the 1912 reporting period, the new home was completed. There would not only be a new home, but a new hospital, barns, blacksmith shop, laundry facility, powerhouse, and a cottage for the farmers. The Odd Fellows Home in Thermalito had all of these facilities and more, but it was nearing its end. None of the home trustees were replaced for the 1912 period, for each had done a superb performance in overseeing the construction of the new facility in Saratoga. No others were even nominated to challenge a single trustee.

The trustees were left with two major goals for the upcoming year: the residents of the Thermalito Home would have to be transferred to Saratoga, and the Thermalito property would have to be sold.

With the new home came new prices. Life Memberships to the home could still be purchased for $1,000; however, the price was increased to $1,500 for those aged 60 to 64 years; for those 55 to 59, the price of a Life Membership was $2,000. Those 65 and older would pay $1,000. Again, a Life Membership was for those members who could not qualify for admission to the facility because they had a sustainable income, but wanted to live at the Odd Fellows home.

In May 1913, the Grand Master was the first to submit his report. Grand Master Charles L. Snyder visited the home in Thermalito two times. The reports on Thermalito were no doubt, brief. The first visit came August 12, 1912. The residents of the home had not yet moved to Saratoga. He made an inspection of the buildings and grounds. Then he

Grand Master Charles L. Snyder (circa 1913).

noted the attitude of the staff: "a general air of expectancy caused by the contemplated removal of the inmates seemed to pervade." It was inevitable there would no longer be an Odd Fellows home in Thermalito.

On the Grand Master's second visit to Thermalito, the scene was very different. By April 28, 1913, the residents had all been transferred to Saratoga. A caretaker of the Thermalito Home property was now in charge. The facility had already been vacated for 5 months.

On November 17, 1912, trustees of the home, John Thompson (president), John Hazlett, D. A. Sinclair, and Fred E. Pierce, along with James W. Harris, Grand Treasurer of the Grand Lodge, and Harry D. Richardson, Grand Secretary of the Grand Lodge, visited the home in Thermalito. They prepared for the morning's move. The arrangements for the residents to be taken by train from Oroville to Congress Junction, the closest station to the new home, had been made by the Grand Treasurer, James W. Harris. There were 133 residents to transport (105 men and 28 women). Of course, there would also be many volunteer chaperones to make the trip.

Before darkness had fallen at the home, the group paid a visit to Patriarchs' Rest, which sat on a high bluff overlooking the Feather River and the town of Oroville. Later in the evening, after dinner, the residents were reminded to be up and ready in the morning for the trip to the new facility. However, before the group broke from the dinner tables, many reflected on the good times spent at the Thermalito Home. On November 18, 1912, at 5:00 the following morning, after breakfast, everyone was taken to the Western Pacific Railroad. The people of Oroville provided automobiles and other means of transportation to move the residents to the train station. At 7:00, everyone boarded the train going to the new home, nearly 200 miles away. There was a grand send-off as many people of the town, including members of the Order, came to bid them farewell.

In Sacramento, the train was switched over to the Southern Pacific Railway. Through the efforts of the Grand Treasurer, James Harris, and the kindness of each railway company, the trip did not cost the odd Fellows anything; it was provided free of charge. In Sacramento, Stockton, and other locations where the train rolled through, Odd Fellows and Rebekahs held greeting signs and stood waving to the residents. The occupants of the train stopped in Stockton for an evening dinner and then resumed their journey to Congress Junction.

When the train finally arrived at the Congress Junction, it was met with "fifty or more autos" donated to carry the residents to the new site. This had been arranged by Home Trustee S. E. Moreland (vice president). The travelers were tired. Many of them required assistance.

The Western Pacific train depot in Oroville, where the residents boarded on November 18, 1912.

There were plenty of volunteers on hand to give assistance. The move went smoothly.

The Grand Master traveled 500 miles away from his schedule of visits near Modoc County just to welcome the residents to their new home.

The property at Thermalito sat awaiting new owners, if any could be found. In 1913, the trustees reported the Loyal Order of Moose wanted the property for a home or school, but the people in Thermalito signed a petition opposing the transaction, ending the deal.

The trustees of the home were busy concentrating their efforts at the new facility; closing out the transactions at Thermalito was slow. The property in Thermalito was comprised of many deeds and needed to be properly handled. The trustees asked the Grand Lodge to consider whether or not the cemetery should remain. The Thermalito property

A group of Odd Fellows waiting for the train at Thermalito after visiting the home on May 13, 1908. The members often visited the home in large groups. This particular visit would have been a week prior to the Grand Lodge session. (Courtesy of the California Historical Society, FN-36560.)

was placed on the market for a sale price of $40,000. The property must have looked like a ghost town. Where there were once hundreds either residing, visiting, or working on the premises, there were none. Only the dead remained.

The deaths reported for the period were as follows: John J. Porter, 73, pleuropneumonia; John Carson, 83, dysentery; Mrs. C. Hash, 73, valvular disease of the heart, congestion of the lungs; Theodore Linck, 80, cerebral hemorrhage, heat prostration; Frederick Gilbert, 78, valvular disease of the heart; W. H. Hillhouse, 86, gastroenteritis, senility, and debility; James Nelson, 65, tubercular meningitis; William Buist, 70, pleuropneumonia; John Tucker, 72, pulmonary tuberculosis, and Mrs. Mary Park, 71, erysipelas—the last inmate to pass away at the Thermalito Home.

Again, the trustees of the home maintained their positions on the board. None were replaced. Their future reports on Thermalito would be minimal.

CHAPTER 17

CLOSING THE DOOR

In 1914, the president or the vice president of the home at various times visited the Thermalito property, entertaining offers to purchase the Odd Fellows home site. The trustees said, "As the time passes the buildings would need attention." They called upon the membership to help find a buyer for the property. This report—or lack thereof—was indicative that nothing was occurring at the old home. The only reason a caretaker had been hired to look after the grounds 2 years earlier was because it was required by the insurance company. In 1915, no report on the old home was offered by either the Grand Master or the trustees of the facility. However, buried in the itemized expenses was a listing of a salary in the amount of $600 for the "caretaker of the old Home." Other than this listing, it would be difficult to determine if the home in Thermalito was still held by the Order.

The 1916 report of the home trustees centered on the death of fellow trustee John Thompson (former president), but there was also mention of the Thermalito property. The trustees were still trying to find a buyer and expressed hope in selling it very soon. The structures, aside from a few minor reports, were reported to be in "splendid condition."

In a 1917 report, and after 4 long years, a Grand Master finally visited the old home property in Thermalito. In short, the half-page report stated that the buildings had become dilapidated. Roofs leaked, trees were dying, and there was a great fire risk. It was costing the Odd Fellows $1,200 a year to maintain the property—with no income return. The Grand Master instructed the trustees to liquidate the property.

In the trustees' report, it was stated the orchards were in "good condition" and that there had been minor repairs to two of the roofs. The buildings were reported to be in fair condition. Nothing to the extent of what the Grand Master had reported was indicated by the trustees of the facility. Once again, the trustees called upon the membership to help sell the property.

On May 14, 1918, the final reports concerning the old home in Thermalito would be offered. The Grand Master reported the property had at long last been sold, with the exception of the cemetery. He also added the cemetery should be cared for by the efforts of the Grand Lodge. There had been many members of the Odd Fellows laid to final rest in Thermalito.

The trustees of the home offered its final report on Thermalito. A buyer had offered to purchase the entire property, including the cemetery, for $5,000. But this amount was later reduced by $250, as the buyer could not guarantee to care for the cemetery, as reported by the trustees:

> "The purchaser would not give us satisfactory assurance that the cemetery plot, which was included in the sale, would be cared for or that bodies of our deceased residents who are buried there would be allowed to remain for a definite time, so this portion, consisting of five acres, was reconvened to the Trustees of the Home for the sum of $250."

After paying expenses, the sale of the Thermalito property netted $4,616.22. That was the end of the home in Thermalito. It would soon fade into only a distant memory.

In 1918, the old home was torn down by the new owner. Eventually, all the structures would be removed. Only the palm trees would remain as evidence for those researching the chronicles of Thermalito and how it grew into a small community by way of an Odd Fellows home.

On June 14, 1919, the Grand Lodge turned over the deed to the cemetery to Oroville Lodge No. 59. In exchange, the Grand Lodge requested Oroville Lodge to "furnish an agreement to take care of the graves."

OFFICE OF THE GRAND SECRETARY

I.O.O.F.

ODD FELLOWS BUILDING
cor. SEVENTH and MARKET STS.

TELEPHONE - MARKET 936

H. D. RICHARDSON,
GRAND SECRETARY

SAN FRANCISCO, CAL.

June 16, 1919

To the N.G., V.G., Officers and Members of Oroville
Lodge, No. 159, I.O.O.F.,
Oroville, Calif.

Dear Sirs and Brothers:

At a meeting of the Board of Trustees of the
Odd Fellows Home held on June 14, 1919, the Board
requested that you beinformed regarding the action taken
at the recent session of the Grand Lodge at which the
Trustees of the Odd Fellows Home were authorized and
empowered to execute a gift deed of the cemetery of the
old Home at Thermalito, to you with the understanding
that Oroville Lodge, No. 59 shall, at all times, care for
and keep in good condition, the graves of our deceased
brothers and sisters interred therein.
The Board desires that you signify for whom you
wish the deed made out to and at the same time suggest that
the deed may be made out to the trustees of your lodge and
their successors in office.
The Board also suggests that you would furnish
an agreement to take care of the graves now in the plot.

Fraternally yours,

Grand Secretary.

A letter from the Odd Fellows Home Board, via the Grand Lodge of California, giving
Oroville Lodge #59 the deed to the cemetery.

CHAPTER 18

THE SUMMATION

The Odd Fellows in California had entered a new phase of its growth process when it decided to establish a home for indigent and aged members. For years, dissension prevailed, as detailed in the annual reports. The trustees of the home regularly contradicted the appointed Special Investigating Committees or a displeased Grand Master in the annual reports. The trustees of the home knew the process better than anyone. They had overseen the development of the facility day in and day out. They were the most familiar members who watched regularly the growth and expansion of the Thermalito Home.

Why were so many reluctant to embrace the home? Change! Remember, it did not matter if the home was in Thermalito, Stockton, Southern California, or anywhere else. At this early stage, caring for the aged members of the Order meant accepting change. It meant adapting to another principle. What was worst of all, it meant dipping into the coffers of the lodges. The membership may have put off the idea of having a home in California for years, which it did, for any one of the cited reasons or all of them collectively. When anything, if only even slightly negative, would come to light, the detractors would magnify the event tenfold. It was an opportunity to cast disparaging remarks.

The initial money donated toward the Thermalito Home had been somewhat coerced. The Grand Lodge had stated it would list by lodge the dollar amount given to the home. That meant if a lodge gave nothing, a zero would follow after its name. Very few lodges wanted to be placed in a vilifying position. This was a brotherhood after all. For the most part, most of the lodges contributed the seed money needed to transform the Belle Vista Hotel into the Odd Fellows Home of Thermalito.

Other factors lent to the continuation of the home in Thermalito. An article concerning the affairs of the home was published and released on April 26, 1899, by the *Oroville Register*, submitted by Oroville Lodge No. 59. The 23-page article strongly defended the home at Thermalito. The lodge went so far as to appoint its own committee to report the facts of the home to the members of the Grand Lodge. In the response made to the members of the Grand Lodge, the Oroville Lodge discredits the Special Home Investigating Committee, which had written a scathing report on the facility. Item by item, the committee tore down the myths and deceit of the Grand Lodge's Special Home Investigating Committee.

As was pointed out by the Odd Fellows from the Oroville Lodge: it was hot in Thermalito, but it was hot almost anywhere in the summer. In general, elderly people seem to expire more often than younger people due to the heat. When a group of aged people are placed together in one location, the death rate will appear much higher for a given period. The detractors who were mostly always on the attack thought the high incidences of deaths were surprising, when, in fact, these were not surprising to the people closest to the home and the doctors that had provided the health care.

An interesting item contained in the appendix of the article printed in the *Oroville Register* was the recorded testimonies of 69 residents. This rare document offers a singular insight to what these people had to say concerning the home. In the statement numbered "3,3," we find the name of William Quayle again. In 1898, when he raised the flag at the home, Quayle was the oldest resident, at 86 years of age.

Three men also played an important role in the establishment of the first home in California. Perhaps without their generosity of donating an uncompleted hotel in a place called Thermalito, a home would not have been started, at least, not until several more years. The three men went in different directions after making their contribution of a near-ready-made home.

Edward W. Fogg and McLaughlin continued growing olives and producing olive oil, where they found success. Fogg also conducted an insurance and loan business. Albert F. Jones eventually served on the home board, serving for several years. They envisioned a colony and probably thought they had failed by not completing the hotel or selling as much acreage as hoped. But today, there is a town of Thermalito because of these men. In November of 1907, after years of various business endeavors, Major Frank McLaughlin, sometimes called "Colonel," committed suicide shortly after murdering his stepdaughter. He cited "the lack of finances" as the trigger; however, after the sale of his estate, there was plenty of money remaining.

The change to accept the home took time. It took about a decade for the membership to accept having a home. Even many of the critical reports offered by the Grand Masters of the 1800s seemed to be less critical in the 1900s. In 1894, when the home property was acquired, it was not the terrible place that it started out to be—not until the following year when the lodges were charged a per capita fee to support the operations of the facility.

Again, this was a new concept to the lodges that were asked to financially support the "new" home at Thermalito. The vast majority of lodges did not have any of their members staying there. Therefore, it is conceivable the lodges not having any members residing at the home would resist paying for the same.

Where much of the membership did not care to watch the home grow month by month, a handful of members believed in the concept of providing a home for California Odd Fellowship. These members expected a challenge of raising funds, fending off negativity, and dealing with occasional setbacks. The trustees of the home were these special members, the positive thinkers. The first elected trustees of the home saw the gradual successes and immense possibilities at Thermalito. When any complaint was lodged by a Grand Master or the eventual Special Home Investigating Committee, it responded to those complaints and dealt with them in a constructive manner. The trustees listened and fixed the perceived problem. The trustees knew all along the home in Thermalito was a well-suited location to have the Odd Fellows home, but it was selfish stubbornness that won out in the end. There was little else the home trustees could do except do as it had been instructed by the Grand Lodge membership and report the facts.

Palms along driveway in 1909. These palm trees still stand today.

This exchange between the trustees and Grand Master and the Special Home Investigating Committee went on for years. As time went by, there were fewer and fewer problems to address. The membership had become used to having a home, as they had been supporting the facility now for years. By the time the property in Saratoga had been purchased, the complaints of Thermalito were very few, if any. The new Saratoga Home had been custom-built by a new, larger membership far removed from initial changes caused by the introduction of a home in its jurisdiction.

Aside from a stately row of palm trees where the Thermalito Home once stood, only the old home cemetery remains. The palm trees are the only reminders of the Odd Fellows home, as most everything else was destroyed by a devastating fire in 1927. Today, even the majority of the Order's membership is unaware of the cemetery, much less the history of the Odd Fellows home in Thermalito. The Odd Fellows were prominent in Thermalito. You might even argue the Odd Fellows had its own little community. Although mostly forgotten, this is a place we call historic.

Today, these palm trees are all that remain at the site of the home.

On top of this bank of the Feather River is the old "Patriarch's Rest" (at right, above), where many of those who died at the home were buried (circa 2008).

Subsequently, there have been approximately 31 additional burials at the cemetery since the home's closing in 1912. After all, it is a cemetery. Over the years, the cemetery has been vandalized. Many of the headstones were tossed over the 80-foot bank into the Feather River below. The headstones were later recovered using scuba divers from the Paradise Dive Center in the nearby town of Paradise, who had volunteered their services. Oroville Lodge No. 59 still maintains the cemetery to this day.

To this day, there have been no other books written of the Odd Fellows home in Thermalito. There has been only a mention that the home existed. This is a memorial to those who lived, died, and were forgotten.

BIBLIOGRAPHY

Boyle, Florence Danforth. *Old Days in Butte*. Association of Northern California Historical Research, 1974.

Executive Committee Golden Jubilee Celebration, I.O.O.F. of California, under supervision of the Book Committee. *Fifty Years of Odd Fellowship in California*. H. S. Crocker Company, San Francisco, 1899.

Gudde, Erwin G. California *Place Names: The Origin and Etymology of Current Geographical Names*. University of California Press, Berkeley and Los Angeles, 1969.

Powell, Benson Mahlon. *The Triple Links or Odd Fellowship Exemplified*. The Triple Link Co., Cherryville, Kansas, 1902.

Proceedings of the California Grand Lodge of the Independent Order of Odd Fellows of the State of California. San Francisco: Joseph Winterburn & Company, Printers and Electrotypers, 1888.

Proceedings of the California Grand Lodge of the Independent Order of Odd Fellows of the State of California. San Francisco: Joseph Winterburn & Company, Books and Job Printers and Electrotypers, 1889.

Proceedings of the California Grand Lodge of the Independent Order of Odd Fellows of the State of California. San Francisco: Joseph Winterburn & Company, Books and Job Printers and Electrotypers, 1890.

Proceedings of the California Grand Lodge of the Independent Order of Odd Fellows of the State of California. San Francisco: Joseph Winterburn & Company, Books and Job Printers and Electrotypers, 1891.

Proceedings of the California Grand Lodge of the Independent Order of Odd Fellows of the State of California. San Francisco: Joseph Winterburn & Company, Books and Job Printers and Electrotypers, 1892.

Proceedings of the California Grand Lodge of the Independent Order of Odd Fellows of the State of California. San Francisco: Joseph Winterburn & Company, Books and Job Printers and Electrotypers, 1893.

Proceedings of the California Grand Lodge of the Independent Order of Odd Fellows of the State of California. San Francisco: Joseph Winterburn & Company, Books and Job Printers and Electrotypers, 1894.

Proceedings of the California Grand Lodge of the Independent Order of Odd Fellows of the State of California. San Francisco: Joseph Winterburn & Company, Books and Job Printers and Electrotypers, 1895.

Proceedings of the California Grand Lodge of the Independent Order of Odd Fellows of the State of California. San Francisco: Joseph Winterburn & Company, Books and Job Printers and Electrotypers, 1896.

Proceedings of the California Grand Lodge of the Independent Order of Odd Fellows of the State of California. San Francisco: Joseph Winterburn & Company, Books and Job Printers and Electrotypers, 1897.

Proceedings of the California Grand Lodge of the Independent Order of Odd Fellows of the State of California. San Francisco: Joseph Winterburn & Company, Printers and Electrotypers, 1898.

Proceedings of the California Grand Lodge of the Independent Order of Odd Fellows of the State of California. San Francisco: Joseph Winterburn & Company, Printers and Electrotypers, 1899.

Proceedings of the California Grand Lodge of the Independent Order of Odd Fellows of the State of California. San Francisco: Joseph Winterburn & Company, Printers and Electrotypers, 1900.

Proceedings of the California Grand Lodge of the Independent Order of Odd Fellows of the State of California. San Francisco: Joseph Winterburn & Company, Printers and Electrotypers, 1901.

Proceedings of the California Grand Lodge of the Independent Order of Odd Fellows of the State of California. San Francisco: Joseph Winterburn & Company, Printers and Electrotypers, 1902.

Proceedings of the California Grand Lodge of the Independent Order of Odd Fellows of the State of California. San Francisco: Joseph Winterburn & Company, Printers and Electrotypers, 1903.

Proceedings of the California Grand Lodge of the Independent Order of Odd Fellows of the State of California. San Francisco: Joseph Winterburn & Company, Printers and Electrotypers, 1904.

Proceedings of the California Grand Lodge of the Independent Order of Odd Fellows of the State of California. San Francisco: Joseph Winterburn & Company, Printers and Electrotypers, 1905.

Proceedings of the California Grand Lodge of the Independent Order of Odd Fellows of the State of California. San Francisco: Joseph Winterburn & Company, Printers and Electrotypers, 1906.

Proceedings of the California Grand Lodge of the Independent Order of Odd Fellows of the State of California. San Francisco: Marshall Press, 1907.

Proceedings of the California Grand Lodge of the Independent Order of Odd Fellows of the State of California. San Francisco: Marshall Press, 1908.

Proceedings of the California Grand Lodge of the Independent Order of Odd Fellows of the State of California. San Francisco: Marshall Press, 1909.

Proceedings of the California Grand Lodge of the Independent Order of Odd Fellows of the State of California. San Francisco: Marshall Press, 1910.

Proceedings of the California Grand Lodge of the Independent Order of Odd Fellows of the State of California. San Francisco: Marshall Press, 1911.

Proceedings of the California Grand Lodge of the Independent Order of Odd Fellows of the State of California. San Francisco: Marshall Press, 1912.

Proceedings of the California Grand Lodge of the Independent Order of Odd Fellows of the State of California. San Francisco: Marshall Press, 1913.

Proceedings of the California Grand Lodge of the Independent Order of Odd Fellows of the State of California. San Francisco: Marshall Press, 1914.

Proceedings of the California Grand Lodge of the Independent Order of Odd Fellows of the State of California. San Francisco: Marshall Press, 1915.

Proceedings of the California Grand Lodge of the Independent Order of Odd Fellows of the State of California. San Francisco: Marshall Press, 1916.

Proceedings of the California Grand Lodge of the Independent Order of Odd Fellows of the State of California. San Francisco: Marshall Press, 1917.

Proceedings of the California Grand Lodge of the Independent Order of Odd Fellows of the State of California. San Francisco: Marshall Press, 1918.

Wolfe, Ida F. *Album of Odd Fellows Homes.* Minneapolis: The Joseph M. Wolfe Company, 1927.

Newspaper Articles

"Odd Fellows Celebration," *Oroville Register* (4 April 1895): 2, col. 3.

"Man Drowns in River," *Oroville Daily Register* (13 October 1904): 1, col. 5.

"Turned Up His Toes: Ended Life In A Bathtub," *Oroville Daily Register* (14 October 1904): 1, col. 3.

"Unknown Man is Run Down By Electric Cars," *Oroville Daily Register* (23 November 1907): 1, col. 4.

"Injuries Prove Fatal To Man Struck By Car," *Oroville Daily Register* (25 November 1907): 1, col. 5.

"Ill And Despondent Inmate Of Thermalito Home Ends His Life," *Oroville Daily Register* (24 October 1907): 1, col. 3 (lower page).

"Aged Woman Tired Of Life," *The Oroville Mercury* (September 14, 1911): 1, col. 1.

"When Medicine Fails, Old Man Cuts Throat," *The Oroville Mercury* (January 24, 1912): 1, col. 3.

Note: The authors are unknown for the newspaper articles.

Miscellaneous

A listing detailing the grave locations and list of names in the Thermalito Cemetery. Compiled by Oroville Eagle Scout, Morgan Price. October, 1986.

*Because each Grand Master serves a one-year term beginning in May, for the purpose of simplicity, only the calendar year in which they submitted their annual reports (at the conclusion of their term) is listed with their images.

APPENDIX

The following images are of a 1913 listing of the Thermalito Home residents who passed away.

LIST OF RESIDENTS

OF THE

Odd Fellows Home of California, at Thermalito, Who Have Died Since Its Organization.

NAME.	AGE	LODGE.	No.	DATE OF ADMISSION.	DATE OF DEATH.
M. MICHELSEN	59	Germania	116	Aug. 24, 1895	Sept. 21, 1895
E D. HERRICK	66	Oustomah	16	Aug. 15, 1895	Sept. 28, 1895
HENRY FRIEDEL	81	Harmony	13	Sept. 14, 1895	Jan. 18, 1896
I C. FATCH	72	Greenville	252	Oct. 1, 1895	Mar. 14, 1896
M. B. SEIFERT	61	Stockton	11	Jan. 4, 1896	July 11, 1896
HERMAN SEIFERT	63	Stockton	11	Jan. 4, 1896	Sept. 1, 1896
DANIEL KNIGHT	68	Mariposa	39	Sept. 13, 1895	Oct. 23, 1896
JOHN N. SMALL	72	Charity	6	May 16, 1896	Nov. 13, 1896
E. B. PALMER	59	El Dorado	8	Aug. 19, 1895	Dec. 29, 1896
HENRY WILSON	85	Wildey	149	Nov. 25, 1895	Jan. 9, 1897
GEORGE ATKINS	67	Brooklyn	46	June 19, 1896	Jan. 21, 1897
HENRY C. HALL	60	University	144	Sept. 16 1895	April 4, 1897
JOHN RULE	85	San Juan	67	Dec. 5, 1896	April 23, 1897
THOMAS CORKLE	68	Greenville	252	Mar. 21, 1896	May 11, 1897
J. B. HOLJE	72	Concordia	122	April 21, 1897	June 18, 1897
MRS. M. C. KEITH	74	Granite	62	Aug. 24, 1895	June 19, 1897
CONRAD MEYER	68	Campo Seco	66	Feb. 7, 1896	July 16, 1897
JOHN W. MCLAIN	69	San Diego	153	Aug. 19, 1895	July 22, 1897
GUILAMO TOGNINI	55	Laguna	224	April 25, 1895	July 31, 1897
ALLEN RIFFAL	65	Greenville	252	Nov. 15, 1895	Aug. 24, 1897
ED. D. BATTURS	72	Templar	17	Aug. 10, 1895	Sept. 13, 1897
GEORGE KLEIN	60	Garden City	142	Sept. 12, 1895	Sept. 17, 1897
JAMES T. CLARK	75	Sacramento	2	July 6, 1897	Oct. 22, 1897
S. R. BULKLEY	73	Abou Ben Adhem	112	July 20, 1896	Oct. 25, 1897
LOUIS WILLIAMS	68	Marion	101	May 18, 1897	Nov. 1, 1897
CLAUS H. BUMAN	81	Franklin	74	Sept. 4, 1895	Nov. 7, 1897
LEONARD BROWN	70	Mayfield	192	June 29, 1898	Aug. 13, 1898
ELIZABETH RANDALL	67	Sonora	10	July 23, 1896	Oct. 27, 1898
SARAH BARNES	70	Channel City	232	June 1, 1897	Dec. 8, 1898
THOMAS WATSON	71	Oriental	45	Sept. 27, 1895	Dec. 12, 1898
E. COOK	67	Charity	6	Jan. 29, 1897	Jan. 6, 1899
HENRY NOLTE	71	University	144	Aug. 17, 1896	Feb. 4, 1899
B. GUINAND	73	Santa Barbara	156	Sept. 17, 1895	Mar. 16, 1899
L. N. SNYDER	68	Abou Ben Adhem	112	Aug. 24, 1895	Aug. 21, 1899
S F. LURVEY	80	Bay View	109	Dec. 27, 1898	Oct. 21, 1899
G. LANDON	74	Industrial	157	July 1, 1897	Oct. 26, 1899
J F. MONHARDT	76	Etna	184	Sept. 29, 1895	Feb. 21, 1900
E. GREGORY	79	San Diego	153	May 8, 1895	Feb. 28, 1900
H. VANCE	73	Rio Vista	180	Dec. 9, 1899	Aug. 3, 1900
CALVIN C. STEVENS	80	Yerba Buena	15	Dec. 11, 1895	Nov. 15, 1900
WILLIAM T. LIGGETT	75	Donner	162	Nov. 30, 1896	Feb. 7, 1901
MRS. H. E. WARNCKE	49	Myrtle	275	Sept. 15, 1895	Feb. 15, 1901
THOMAS S. WOOD	71	Riverside	282	July 8, 1898	May 11, 1901
JAMES CONWAY	65	Santa Barbara	156	Dec. 24, 1895	June 29, 1901
CATHERINE HERR	86	Brownsville	283	Feb. 11, 1897	July 13, 1901
WILLIAM SUNDEMEYER	72	Independence	158	Sept. 10, 1895	July 18, 1901
JAMES DAVIS, P. G.	76	California	1	Jan. 20, 1896	July 27, 1901
CHARLES COOK	74	Franklin	74	Dec. 8, 1900	Nov. 9, 1901
ERNEST DUNKER	82	Germania	116	Oct. 1, 1898	Nov. 14, 1901
WILLIAM QUAYLE	87	Camptonville	307	June 24, 1896	Dec. 6, 1901
ADAM HOFFMAN	71	Honey Lake	223	Nov. 19, 1897	Dec. 9, 1901
JOSEPH SILVA	61	Plumas	88	Jan. 22, 1897	Feb. 2, 1902
W. S. HINMAN	76	Montezuma	172	Nov. 18, 1896	Feb. 12, 1902
O. H. TUFTS	73	San Juan	67	Aug. 31, 1895	Mar. 2, 1902
J W. ASHTON	69	Morning Star	20	Nov. 22, 1898	Mar. 10, 1902
F. M. DILLIAN	71	Ione	51	July 23, 1896	Mar. 31, 1902
JOHN YOCCO	61	Franco-Italian	242	Aug. 10, 1900	May 4, 1902
JOHN W. SADLER	64	Donner	162	Feb. 13, 1900	June 24, 1902
JOHN W. BARNES	75	Channel City	232	June 1, 1897	Aug. 6, 1902

APPENDIX

DIED AT THE HOME.—Continued.

NAME.	AGE	LODGE.	No.	DATE OF ADMISSION.	DATE OF DEATH.
MARGARET MASON	69	Charity	6	Nov. 7, 1895	Nov. 2, 1902
CARLOS VINCENT	81	Mokelumne	44	Dec. 20, 1897	Dec. 2, 1902
ELLEN GIBNEY	67	Fidelity	222	Mar. 18, 1897	Jan. 8, 1903
RUDOLPH DEKRUSE	76	Placer	38	Jan. 24, 1899	Jan. 25, 1903
ANDREW GARRITY	64	Magnolia	29	Sept. 18, 1899	Mar. 29, 1903
JAMES WATSON	70	Welcome	209	Dec. 13, 1902	April 2, 1903
HORACE GATES	85	California	1	Feb. 12, 1896	April 29, 1903
JOHN A. FORTADO	76	Mt. Horeb	58	July 10, 1897	April 29, 1903
T. N. MOODY	70	Napa	18	Oct. 6, 1896	June 28, 1903
D. A. McPHEE*	74	San Juan	67	Feb. 11, 1897	July 24, 1903
WILLIAM MOSS	82	Mountain	14	Nov. 11, 1902	Oct. 16, 1903
ALFRED HIMES	74	Mountain Vale	140	Feb. 14, 1901	Oct. 18, 1903
EMILY J. McDONALD	76	Golden State	216	June 2, 1900	Jan. 18, 1904
CHARLES J. WARNER*	73	Eureka	4	Jan. 21, 1897	Mar. 21, 1904
FREDERICK HARTLEB	82	Petaluma	30	Dec. 16, 1895	Mar. 24, 1904
JOHN MULLIN	66	El Dorado	8	Aug. 3, 1903	April 18, 1904
AMOS BALDWIN	82	Calistoga	227	Dec. 13, 1897	May 1, 1904
WILLIAM T. AZBILL	74	Anaheim	199	Nov. 4, 1895	May 11, 1904
FRED. DECKER	77	Concordia	122	June 23, 1895	May 22, 1904
FRANK H. DEIDELL	75	Forest City	32	Feb. 14, 1904	May 26, 1904
WILLIAM A. IRWIN	81	Sutter Creek	31	Mar. 18, 1900	June 20, 1904
LENA FORTRO	72	Parker	124	April 2, 1902	July 11, 1904
LOUIS KASELAU	80	Sharon	86	Mar. 25, 1898	July 27, 1904
FRANK G. GUILD	80	Oustomah	16	Oct. 24, 1897	Aug. 13, 1904
THOMAS BENSON	76	Golden Gate	204	Aug. 30, 1895	Aug. 29, 1904
MARY A. CHRISTMAN	83	Plumas	88	Feb. 10, 1901	Sept. 28, 1904
FREDERICK C. WAITE*	77	Templar	17	Jan. 20, 1902	Sept. 29, 1904
ELIZABETH D. MILLER	75	Yerba Buena	15	June 15, 1900	Oct. 6, 1904
HORACE A. PORTER	58	Four Creeks	94	Sept. 12, 1904	Oct. 12, 1904
FRANCIS A. MILLER	75	Yerba Buena	15	Mar. 2, 1898	Oct. 13, 1904
LEOPOLD WELTSCH	69	Garden City	142	April 12, 1902	Oct. 19, 1904
CHARLES A. WIKMAN	51	Placer	38	April 1, 1903	Nov. 1, 1904
JOHN BINNING	66	Mistletoe	54	Sept. 16, 1895	Nov. 18, 1904
JAMES H. BISHOP	76	California	1	Nov. 18, 1903	Feb. 19, 1905
WILLIAM H. MASON	71	Charity	6	Nov. 2, 1895	Mar. 5, 1905
JOHN ALEXANDER	76	Inyo	301	Nov. 11, 1901	Mar. 6, 1905
CHARLES P. WOLCOTT	77	Abou Ben Adhem	112	June 1, 1897	Mar. 30, 1905
HANS TECKLENBERG	81	Mistletoe	54	April 6, 1901	April 24, 1905
GEORGE W. KNEEDLER	83	Garden City	142	Jan. 16, 1905	April 29, 1905
JOHN RUTAN	85	Lodi	259	June 6, 1896	May 10, 1905
PETER NOEL	83	Chico	113	Dec. 11, 1899	June 26, 1905
CHARLES L. KNOWLES	79	Sacramento	2	June 9, 1904	June 28, 1905
WILLIAM G. DINSMORE	83	Oakland	118	May 14, 1904	July 11, 1905
JOHN DESOMBRE	80	Indian Valley	136	Nov. 6, 1899	July 20, 1905
WILLIAM T. HENDRICK	83	Pacheco	117	Dec. 7, 1904	July 21, 1905
NANNIE BECKER	82	Germania	116	July 6, 1905	Aug. 9, 1905
LEONARD CURTIS	81	Branciforte	96	Sept. 12, 1901	Sept. 2, 1905
MARY HILL	69	Olive	81	Aug. 12, 1905	Sept. 7, 1905
H. SCHUMACHER	73	Union	48	June 24, 1896	Oct. 2, 1905
H. F. SCHRIERHOLD	78	Concordia	122	Nov. 25, 1904	Oct. 4, 1905
ADAM GOLDSMITH	75	El Dorado	8	Nov. 30, 1896	Oct. 6, 1905
EMMA JANSEN	76	Donner	162	Sept. 13, 1900	Oct. 8, 1905
F. P. ANDERSON	62	Morse	257	April 2, 1903	Oct. 23, 1905
WILLIAM M. DENIG	75	Stockton	11	July 19, 1905	Nov. 5, 1905
GEORGE B. ZAISS	80	Mineral	106	Dec. 10, 1904	Nov. 12, 1905
ALJONETTE ENNIS*	72	Progressive	134	Sept. 24, 1903	Nov. 20, 1905
PHILLIP LUNNEY	68	San Pablo	43	Aug. 16, 1898	Nov. 24, 1905
C. F. H. KOCH	75	Western Addition	285	Jan. 7, 1896	Dec. 15, 1905
R. W. HATHEWAY	77	Oakdale	228	Feb. 11, 1902	Dec. 28, 1905
ISAAC J. DOTY	73	Sutter Creek	31	Dec. 8, 1904	Jan. 1, 1906
WILLIAM WEIR†	73	Thistle (Penn.)	512	Jan. 12, 1904	Feb. 10, 1906
CHARLES SHIRLEY	66	Mound	166	Mar. 16, 1896	Feb. 21, 1906
SAMUEL GUTHRIE	77	Presidio	334	May 24, 1905	Feb. 22, 1906
J. H. CURTIS	73	Branciforte	96	May 11, 1905	Mar. 19, 1906
JOHN MACFARLANE	87	Friendship	150	Sept. 3, 1905	May 24, 1906
MATHEW JANSEN	83	Donner	162	Feb. 15, 1900	June 20, 1906
GEO. W HERRON	76	Buena Vista	268	Nov. 12, 1895	July 7, 1906

DIED AT THE HOME.—*Continued.*

NAME.	AGE	LODGE.	No.	DATE OF ADMISSION.	DATE OF DEATH.
HANS PETER NELSON....	59	(Defunct)........	....	Aug. 29, 1895	July 12, 1906
GEO. W. RICHISON......	77	Morning Star	20	Dec. 24, 1895	Aug. 2, 1906
ADAM VOLK	72	Mariposa	39	July 20, 1899	Aug. 9, 1906
JANE MILLNER	75	Mt. Horeb	58	Sept. 12, 1905	Sept. 27, 1906
JOHN PETER BAETTGE ...	76	Germania	116	Dec. 8, 1900	Oct. 12, 1906
WILLIAM BECKER	89	Germania	116	July 6, 1905	Nov. 10, 1906
RILEY SINGLETARY......	78	North Butte	267	Feb. 17, 1904	Nov. 15, 1906
MATTHEW PLEMING	64	Jackson	36	Feb. 12, 1906	Dec. 1, 1906
JOHN JACOB WAGNER ...	75	Tuolumne	44	Sept. 14, 1900	Dec. 12, 1906
WM. C. WILKERSON	80	Osceola	215	Dec. 3, 1896	Jan. 24, 1907
HARVEY TURNER	81	Plumas	88	May 22, 1896	Jan. 27, 1907
SUSAN DAINS	74	Memento........	37	April 12, 1902	Feb. 8, 1907
J. S. BARNES	79	Sacramento	2	Jan. 24, 1899	Feb. 22, 1907
JOSHUA WEBB..........	80	Mokelumne......	44	Nov. 12, 1895	April 6, 1907
TAMMA HURD..........	75	Bay View	109	Jan. 9, 1906	May 10, 1907
JOS. D. BURDICK.......	74	Yerba Buena....	15	April 6, 1907	May 11, 1907
EPENETUS WALLACE.....	84	San Lorenzo.....	147	Jan. 14, 1907	June 3, 1907
WILLIAM ROBERTS......	75	Auburn.........	7	Nov. 8, 1895	June 10, 1907
JAMES E. PAYTON.......	77	Red Bluff.......	76	Boarder	June 22, 1907
H. P. CHRISTENSEN.....	81	Camptonville....	307	Dec. 3, 1897	Aug. 12, 1907
WM. L. McKAY.........	77	Fountain........	198	July 17, 1906	Aug. 20, 1907
ASA B. JENNY.........	65	America.........	385	May 14, 1907	Oct. 24, 1907
ANN STARTIN..........	65	Enterprise.......	298	June 28, 1904	Nov. 11, 1907
GEO. W. WILLIAMSON ...	74	Olive..........	81	Nov. 11, 1907	Nov. 18, 1907
GUSTAV EYMAT........	66	Franco American.	207	Oct. 23, 1907	Nov. 24, 1907
FRANCIS W. PEABODY....	77	Escondido	344	Dec. 3, 1896	Dec. 2, 1907
JOS. H. MITCHELL.......	86	Adin...........	273	June 13, 1905	Dec. 5, 1907
D. D. GREEN..........	85	Mountain Brow ..	82	Sept. 15, 1899	Dec 8, 1907
AMOS J. ROSS	78	University......	144	May 18, 1903	Dec. 12, 1907
SUMNER McCAUSLAND....	75	Oustomah........	16	Jan. 9, 1906	Dec. 18, 1907
LOUIS H. NOLTE.......	82	Pacific..........	155	Aug. 12, 1905	Dec. 19, 1907
CHAUNCY LANGDON.....	80	Onward.........	380	Jan. 10, 1905	Dec. 29, 1907
THOMAS W. EDWARDS ...	72	Alturas.........	80	Jan. 14, 1907	Jan. 8, 1908
F. CHARLES HAHN	78	Excelsior.......	310	July 14, 1906	Feb. 4, 1908
GEO. W. CARSWELL.....	80	Apollo..........	123	Oct. 12, 1904	Feb. 11, 1908
RIX A. JOHNSTON.......	73	Apollo..........	123	Mar. 12, 1903	Feb. 13, 1908
ANDREW F. BROWN......	72	Phoenix.........	239	Mar. 26, 1899	Feb. 13, 1908
AUGUST BANSCH........	73	Hermann........	145	Nov. 3, 1902	Feb. 16, 1908
J. OSCAR TAINTER*.....	83	Forest City......	32	Jan. 6, 1908	May 3, 1908
RICHARD PRYOR........	65	Sutter Creek.....	31	April 24, 1897	June 4, 1908
THOMAS JARVIS.........	72	Porter..........	272	Jan. 21, 1899	June 6, 1908
ROBERT BANDURANT.....	81	Grafton.........	293	July 18, 1905	June 20, 1908
JONATHAN H. PAGE.....	78	Covenant	73	April 7, 1906	July 1, 1908
CHARLES SCHROEDER....	85	San Lorenzo	147	June 24, 1896	July 12. 1908
AZUBA E. FREEMAN*....	79	Santa Ana.......	236	Sept. 17, 1906	July 10, 1908
ISAAC BAKER	80	Escondido	344	Jan. 29, 1898	Oct. 19, 1908
OLE T. TOBIAS........	78	Mountain Rose..	26	Mar. 19, 1905	Oct. 24, 1908
JOHN B. THOMPSON.....	57	Garden City.....	142	Dec. 9, 1905	Nov. 25, 1908
CORNELIUS REYNOLDS....	82	Unity...........	131	Sept. 16, 1907	Dec. 17, 1908
A. W. ESKRIDGE.......	80	Sacramento.....	2	Sept. 17, 1906	Dec. 21, 1908
MARY E. PRICE nee HANER.	73	El Dorado.......	8	June 8, 1903	Dec. 21, 1908
H. C. BAKER.........	79	Long Beach.....	390	Sept. 14, 1908	Dec. 21, 1908
MORRIS MARKS.........	73	Oroville.........	59	Nov. 9, 1908	Jan. 10. 1909
EDWARD PRICE.........	72	Branciforte......	96	July 14, 1906	Feb. 9, 1909
SAMUEL A. LAINE......	79	Telegraph.......	79	Sept. 27, 1905	Mar. 10, 1909
SAMUEL CRADY EDWARDS.	82	Rio Vista	180	Oct. 24, 1900	April 25, 1909
CHARLES FRANK LARAMIE	79	Los Angeles.....	35	Aug. 22, 1895	April 28, 1909
GUSTAV LUEDERS	66	Germania	116	May 20, 1905	May 4, 1909
HENRY HORTON........	83	Bay View	109	Mar. 5, 1901	June 5, 1909
FRANZ SCHMAUSS........	85	Germania.......	116	July 14, 1906	June 19, 1909
HUGH MONTGOMERY.....	71	Adin...........	273	May 15, 1909	July 7, 1909
EDWARD HOPES........	73	Petaluma........	30	Nov. 9, 1908	July 17, 1909
CORNELIUS N. GRAY.....	89	Oriental........	45	April 11, 1908	Aug. 7. 1909
SAMUEL P. JARNIGAN ...	73	Anniversary	85	Aug. 8, 1908	Aug. 21, 1909
THOMAS RUTTER.......	76	Templar.........	17	July 18, 1900	Aug. 21, 1909
GEORGE B. DENSMORE...	82	Apollo.........	123	June 8, 1908	Sept. 8, 1909
EUNICE E. BRIGGS	91	El Dorado	8	June 23, 1908	Sept. 15, 1909
ISAAC W. BARBER	72	Sacramento	2	April 6, 1907	Oct. 8, 1909

DIED AT THE HOME—*Continued.*

NAME.	AGE	LODGE.	No.	DATE OF ADMISSION.	DATE OF DEATH.
JOSEPH D. SPENCER	79	California	1	July 14, 1906	Oct. 8, 1909
WILLIAM J. NICHOLSON	87	Lupyoma	173	April 12, 1902	Oct. 15, 1909
HENRY PROVOST	69	River	256	Feb. 8, 1909	Oct. 25, 1909
JOHN KEAN	76	Golden State	216	May 16, 1904	Oct. 26, 1909
EPHRAIM J. McCOURTNEY	87	Templar	17	Oct. 12, 1908	Nov. 16, 1909
*ANTOINETTE L. BURDICK	76	Yerba Buena	15	Sept. 14, 1908	
PETER DEVAULT	76	Anniversary	85	Oct. 28, 1902	Dec. 26, 1909
JAMES McGRANAHAN	84	Oroville	59	April 11, 1904	Jan. 13, 1910
HERMAN HAKE	81	Volcano	25	April 7, 1906	Jan. 14, 1910
CHARLES WENTWORTH	85	Memento	37	Nov. 9, 1908	Jan. 15, 1910
EDMUND G. BURGER	83	Woodland	111	April 21, 1897	Jan. 25, 1910
JOHN PATTERSON	84	Scio	102	Nov. 6, 1903	Mar. 9, 1910
GEORGE W. ANDREWS	64	Mistletoe	54	Nov. 2, 1909	May 7, 1910
JOSIAH LIBBY BANGS	72	Livermore	219	July 23, 1909	May 9, 1910
B. B. JACKSON	96	Porter	272	Sept. 16, 1907	June 19, 1910
E. WARNEKE	69	Myrtle	275	Sept. 16, 1895	June 20, 1910
JOHN A. HOLM	70	Morse	257	June 18, 1910	July 30, 1910
JAMES G. DICKINSON	74	Cosmopolitan	194	July 14, 1906	Sept. 8, 1910
SAMUEL G. McPHERSON	82	Alta	205	Aug. 13, 1910	Sept. 28, 1910
DAVID CORDER GLENN	80	Vacaville	83	Nov. 13, 1909	Oct. 9, 1910
ROSEANNA BAUMAN	90	Anniversary	85	July 2, 1905	Oct. 15, 1910
JAMES J. WARNER	57	Santa Rosa	53	June 30, 1910	Oct. 20, 1910
AMANDA STRATTON	73	Templar	17	April 10, 1909	Oct. 20, 1910
WILLIAM B. KIMBALL	53	Los Angeles	35	Jan. 24, 1910	Nov. 4, 1910
SARAH E. MORRIS	74	Pleasanton	255	Nov. 12, 1906	Nov. 16, 1910
JAMES W. ARCHIBALD	78	Alta	205	Jan. 11, 1909	Dec. 26, 1910
MINERVA JANE REED	57	Merced	208	Jan. 27, 1910	Dec. 29, 1910
JOSHUA ALBRIGHT	81	Mokelumne	44	July 9, 1910	Jan. 6, 1911
JOHN FOSTER	84	Harbor	253	June 24, 1896	Jan. 14, 1911
ANNA WUTHRICH	61	Hermann	145	April 1, 1910	Feb. 3, 1911
JOHN KIMBERLIN	74	Red Bluff	76	Oct. 3, 1909	Feb. 21, 1911
DANIEL SUTHERLAND	83	Chico	113	April 6, 1907	Feb. 28, 1911
HUGH WALKER	68	Marin	200	Nov. 9, 1908	Feb. 28, 1911
JAMES McCURRY	80	Osceola	215	Mar. 3, 1896	Mar. 14, 1911
WILLIAM D. YOUNG	81	Morse	257	June 25, 1910	Mar. 27, 1911
CHAS. BOWMAN	73	Fountain	198	Nov. 17, 1905	June 11, 1911
HARRIET L. CARSWELL	72	Apollo	123	Oct. 12, 1904	June 11, 1911
WM. J. HILL	75	Olive	81	Aug. 11, 1905	June 22, 1911
*BAPTISTA PAPA	72	Oustomah	16	Jan. 14, 1911	June 25, 1911
ELLEN F. McGOWAN	78	California	1	Aug. 11, 1899	July 15, 1911
P. H. McINTOSH	79	Chico	113	July 21, 1903	July 15, 1911
WALTER C. BATES	77	Telegraph	79	Sept. 26, 1904	Aug. 23, 1911
FRANCIS F. GALERIA	58	Union	48	June 11, 1910	Aug. 25, 1911
AMON J. ROSS	85	Campo Seco	66	May 14, 1901	Aug. 25, 1911
BABETTE HAHN	80	Excelsior	310	July 14, 1906	Sept. 14, 1911
MARIE WALTON	85	Elk Grove	274	Sept. 14, 1908	Sept. 17, 1911
†SAMUEL J. FILER	79	Solano	22	Jan. 14, 1911	Sept. 23, 1911
W. D. SAFFORY	81	Shasta	57	Oct. 12, 1903	Oct. 13, 1911
MARK PARKER	78	Coulterville	104	April 6, 1907	Oct. 18, 1911
ELIZA HART	83	Golden Gate	204	Jan. 21, 1899	Nov. 2, 1911
†MICHAEL M. O'BRIEN	74	Abou Ben Adhem	112	May 11, 1911	Nov. 18, 1911
ELLEN DUGAN	75	California	1	Jan. 11, 1909	Dec. 22, 1911
EBENEZER BIGGS	85	Napa	18	Nov. 2, 1905	Jan. 6, 1912
MARTHA J. BRADLEY	78	Livermore	219	June 22, 1905	Jan. 13, 1912
MATILDA R. TUFTS	94	San Juan	67	Aug. 31, 1895	Jan. 14, 1912
WILLIAM R. KNIGHT	82	Mariposa	39	Oct. 18, 1895	Jan. 24, 1912
WM. B. OVERTON	54	Nacimiento	340	May 11, 1908	Jan. 31, 1912
MICHAEL FINNEY	81	Ione	51	Feb. 20, 1897	Feb. 28, 1912
JOHN J. PORTER	73	Wildey	149	June 16, 1903	June 30, 1912
JOHN CARSON	83	Jefferson	98	May 22, 1898	July 10, 1912
CATHERINE V. HASH	73	Westminster	72	July 15, 1907	July 12, 1912
THEODOR LINCK	80	Cosmopolitan	194	Sept. 30, 1910	July 17, 1912
FREDERICK GILBERT	78	Yerba Buena	15	Sept. 11, 1909	July 25, 1912
WM. H. HILLHOUSE	86	Olive	81	Dec. 9, 1907	Sept. 21, 1912
JAMES NELSON	65	Alta	205	April 13, 1912	Sept. 22, 1912
WILLIAM BUIST	70	Templar	17	Aug. 21, 1895	Sept. 28, 1912
JOHN TUCKER	72	Marion	101	Mar. 28, 1905	Oct. 21, 1912

DIED AT THE HOME—*Concluded.*

NAME.	AGE	LODGE.	NO.	DATE OF ADMISSION.	DATE OF DEATH.
MARY J. PARK	71	Merced	208	April 16, 1906	Nov. 11, 1912
FRANCIS M. NELL	74	Four Creeks	94	June 8, 1912	Nov. 28, 1912
MARY E. MITCHELL	80	Rainbow Reb	97	April 13, 1912	Dec. 24, 1912
MARY A. CAFFALL	78	California	1	July 14, 1906	Dec. 25, 1912
ROBT. H. STRASBURG	78	Etna	184	Sept. 11, 1909	Dec. 29, 1912
GEORGE DIXON	81	Orion	189	May 11, 1912	Jan. 1, 1913
CHAS. F. SMITH	81	San Pablo	43	June 13, 1896	Jan. 9, 1913
ABRAM VAN CAMP	82	Memento	37	April 8, 1902	Jan. 12, 1913
JAMES McCAULEY	85	Ione	51	March 9, 1912	Feb. 11, 1913
JOHN S. REED	83	Yerba Buena	15	Jan. 6, 1908	Feb. 13, 1913
JOHN B. TUPPER	84	Petaluma	30	Nov. 13, 1909	Mar. 2, 1913

*Died while absent on leave.   †Life member.

The images that follow next are a detailed listing of those buried at the Oroville Odd Fellows Cemetery (once called "Patriarchs' Rest"). In 1986, this list was created by Eagle Scout Morgan Price.

Odd Fellows Cemetery (Oroville Lodge No. 59, I.O.O.F.) Oroville (Thermalito), California on 7th St.

page 1

Main Section

Name	Lodge	Site		Date of Death	Birthplace
Mc Farland, Celia	None Listed	Row 1	# 1	6/18/1952	None Listed
Hicks, Rufus	None Listed	Row 1	# 2	1935	None Listed
Hicks, Nancy	None Listed	Row 1	# 2	1950	None Listed
Vaughn, Silas Josia	Odd Fellow Portola # 427	Row 1	# 3	11/13/1935	None Listed
Vaughn, Martha	Rebekah Portola # 339	Row 1	# 4	4/27/1938	None Listed
Harrison, Lewis M	Odd Fellow Dubuque # 125	Row 1	# 5	6/3/1945	Pennsylvania
Tucker Jr., John	Odd Fellow Marion # 101	Row 2	# 1	10/21/1912	None Listed
Buist, William	Odd Fellow Templar # 17	Row 2	# 2	9/28/1912	None Listed
Nelson, James	Odd Fellow Alta # 205	Row 2	# 3	9/22/1912	None Listed
Hash, Catherine	Rbekah Westminister # 78	Row 2	# 4	7/12/1912	None Listed
Finney, Michael	Odd Fellow Ione # 51	Row 2	# 5	2/28/1912	Ireland
Knight, William R.	Odd Fellow Mariposa # 39	Row 2	# 6	1/14/1912	Virginia
Bradley, Martha J.	Rebekah Livermore # 219	Row 2	# 7	1/14/1912	Indiana
Dugan, Ellen	Rebekah California # 1	Row 2	# 8	12/22/1911	England
Mc Intosh, Perry	Odd Fellow Chico # 113	Row 2	# 9	7/15/1911	New York
Bowman, Charles	Odd Fellow Fountain # 198	Row 2	# 10	6/11/1911	Sweden
Walker, Hugh	Odd Fellow Marion # 200	Row 2	# 11	3/3/1911	Nova Scotia
Morris, Sarah E.	Rebekah Pleasanton # 255	Row 2	# 12	11/16/1910	Ohio
Bauman, Roseanne	Rebekah Anniversary # 85	Row 2	# 13	10/15/1919	Ireland
Mc Pherson, Samuel	Odd Fellow Alta # 205	Row 2	# 14	9/28/1910	New Brunswick
Holm, John A.	Odd Fellow Morse # 257	Row 2	# 15	7/13/1910	Sweden
Mc Grananhan, James	Odd Fellow Oroville # 59	Row 2	# 16	1/13/1910	Pennsylvania
Nicholson, William	Odd Fellow Lupyoma # 173	Row 2	# 17	10/15/1909	Delaware
Rutter, Thomas	Odd Fellow Templar # 17	Row 2	# 18	8/21/1909	Nova Scotia
Biggs, Evenezer	Odd Fellow Napa # 118	Row 3	# 1	6/6/1912	Pennsylvania
Kimball, William	Odd Fellow Los Angleles # 35	Row 3	# 2	11/4/1910	Massachusetts
Walton, Maria	Rebekah Elk Grove # 2	Row 3	# 3	9/17/1911	Vermont
Gowan, Ellen	Rebekah California # 1	Row 3	# 4	7/15/1911	Massachusetts
Reynolds, Cornelius	Odd Fellow Unity # 131	Row 3	# 5	12/16/1908	England
Startin, Ann	Rebekah Enterprize # 298	Row 3	# 6	11/11/1907	Ireland
Turner, Harvey	Odd Fellow Plumas # 88	Row 3	# 7	2/15/1907	Indiana
Curtis, James P.G.	Odd Fellow Francifort # 96	Row 3	# 8	3/19/1906	Canada
Porter, Horace A.	Odd Fellow Four Creek # 84	Row 3	# 9	10/22/1904	Canada
Bishop, James H.	Odd Fellow California # 1	Row 3	# 10	2/19/1905	Rhode Island
Wilcott, Chas P.G.	Odd Fellow Abouden Adhen # 112	Row 3	# 11	3/30/1905	Massachusetts
Knowles, Chas L.	Odd Fellow Sacramento # 2	Row 3	# 12	6/28/1905	Pennsylvania
Tecklenberg, Hans	Odd Fellow Misletoe # 54	Row 3	# 13	4/24/1905	Germany
Guild, Frank P.G.	Odd Fellow Oastaman # 16	Row 3	# 14	8/13/1904	New York
Miller. Francis A.	Rebekah Yerba Buena # 15	Row 3	# 15	10/13/1904	New York
Weltsch, Leopold	Odd Fellow Garden City # 142	Row 3	# 16	10/19/1904	Prussia
Shirley, Chas	Odd Fellow Mound # 166	Row 3	# 17	2/21/1906	Tennessee
Gilbert, Frederick	Odd Fellow Yerba Buena # 15	Row 4	# 1	7/25/1912	None Listed
Archibald, Jas W.	Odd Fellow Alta # 205	Row 4	# 2	12/26/1910	Scotland
Mc Curry, James	Odd Fellow Osceola # 215	Row 4	# 3	3/14/1911	North Carolina
Baker, H. G. N.G.	Odd Fellow Long Beach # 390	Row 4	# 4	12/21/1908	Massachusetts
Edwards, Thomas	Odd Fellow Alturas # 80	Row 4	# 5	1/8/1908	Wales
Wallace, Epenetus	Odd Fellow Lerenzo # 147	Row 4	# 6	6/13/1907	New Jersey
Wagner, John Jacob	Odd Fellow Tuolume # 21	Row 4	# 7	12/12/1906	Germany
Mac Farlane, John	Odd Fellow Friendship # 150	Row 4	# 8	5/24/1906	Scotland
Binning, John	Odd Fellow Misletoe # 54	Row 4	# 9	11/18/1904	Germany
Wikman, Chas A.	Odd Fellow Placer # 138	Row 4	# 10	11/1/1904	Finland
Alexander, John P.G.	Odd Fellow Inyo # 301	Row 4	# 11	3/6/1905	Tennessee

Main Section

page 2

Name	Lodge	Site	Date of Death	Birthplace
Noel, Peter	Odd Fellow Chico # 113	Row 4 # 12	6/26/1905	Ohio
Corkle, Thomas	Odd Fellow Greenville # 252	Row 4 # 13	5/11/1897	Isle Of Man
Dinsmore, William G.	Odd Fellow Oakland # 118	Row 4 # 14	7/11/1905	Mane
Benson, Thomas A.	Odd Fellow Golden State # 204	Row 4 # 15	8/29/1904	Denmark
Miller, Elizabeth D.	Rebekah Yerba Buena # 15	Row 4 # 16	10/6/1904	Massachusetts
Ipsen, Peter J. P.G.	Odd Fellow Fountain # 198	Row 4 # 17	11/1/1904	Denmark
Guthrie, Samuel P.G.	Odd Fellow Presidio # 334	Row 4 # 18	2/22/1906	New York
Wuthrich, Anna	Rebekah Nerman # 145	Row 5 # 1	2/3/1911	Germany
Kean, John	Odd Fellow Golden State # 216	Row 5 # 2	10/26/1909	England
Hahn, Babette	Wife	Row 5 # 3	9/14/1911	Germany
Hann, Charles	Odd Fellow Excelsior #310	Row 5 # 4	2/14/1908	Germany
Mitchell, Jos P.G.	Odd Fellow Adin # 173	Row 5 # 5	12/5/1907	Ohio
Barne, J. S.	Odd Fellow Sacramento #2	Row 5 # 6	2/21/1907	New York
Nelson, Hans Peter	Grand Lodge of California (S.F.)	Row 5 # 7	7/12/1906	Denmark
Gates, Horace	Odd Fellow California # 1	Row 5 # 8	4/29/1903	Massachusetts
Forthado, John	Odd Fellow Mount. Horeb # 38	Row 5 # 9	4/29/1903	Portugal
Moss, William P.G.	Odd Fellow Mountain # 14	Row 5 #10	10/16/1903	England
Moody, Timothy P.G.	Odd Fellow Napa # 118	Row 5 # 11	6/28/1902	Tennessee
Warner, Chas A.	Odd Fellow Eureka # 4	Row 5 # 12	3/21/1904	New York
Hartleb, Frederich	Odd Fellow Petaluma # 30	Row 5 # 13	3/24/1904	Germany
Mullins, John	Odd Fellow El Dorado # 8	Row 5 # 14	4/18/1904	Tennessee
Decker, Fred	Odd Fellow Condordia # 122	Row 5 # 15	5/22/1904	Germany
Fortro, Lena	Rebekah Parker # 124	Row 5 # 16	7/14/1904	Germany
Devault, Peter	Odd Fellow Anniversary # 85	Row 6 # 1	7/14/1909	Pennsylvania
Spencer, Jos D. P.G.	Odd Fellow California # 1	Row 6 # 2	10/8/1909	England
Jarnigan, Samuel P.G.	Odd Fellow Anniversary # 85	Row 6 # 3	8/21/1909	Tennessee
Carswell, Hattie L.	Wife	Row 6 # 4	6/11/1911	New York
Carswell, George W.	Odd Fellow Appollo # 123	Row 6 # 5	2/10/1908	Hew Hamshire
Green, D. D. P.G.	Odd Fellow Mount. Brow # 82	Row 6 # 6	12/8/1907	New York
Burdick, Jos D.	Odd Fellow Yerba Buena # 15	Row 6 # 7	5/11/1907	Rhode Island
Richison, George D.	Odd Fellow Morning Star # 20	Row 6 # 8	8/2/1906	New York
Snyder, L. N.	Odd Fellow Abouben Adhen # 112	Row 6 # 9	8/21/1899	New York
Landon, George P.G.	Odd Fellow Industrial # 157	Row 6 # 10	10/26/1899	New York
Monrardt, John F.	Odd Fellow Etna # 184	Row 6 # 11	2/21/1900	Germany
Liggett, William T. P.G.	Odd Fellow Donner # 162	Row 6 # 12	2/7/1901	Missouri
Sundermeyer, William P.G.	Odd Fellow Independence # 158	Row 6 # 13	7/18/1901	Germany
Cook, Charles P.G.	Odd Fellow Franklin # 74	Row 6 # 14	11/9/1901	Germany
Azbill, William T.	Odd Fellow Anaheim # 199	Row 6 # 15	5/11/1904	Missouri
Deidell, Frank H. P.G.	Odd Fellow Forest City # 32	Row 6 # 16	5/26/1904	Germany
Kaselou, Louis	Odd Fellow Sharon # 86	Row 6 # 17	7/27/1904	Germany
Forker, Reverend C. H.	Odd Fellow Hilton # 312	Row 7 # 1	6/8/1931	Virginia
Baker, Earl C.	None Listed	Row 7 # 2	3/31/1921	Virginia
Burger, Edmund G.	Odd Fellow Woodland # 111	Row 7 # 3	6/25/1910	Pennsylvania
Densmore, George B.	Odd Fellow Apollo # 123	Row 7 # 4	9/8/1909	Massachusetts
Montgomery, Hugh P.G.	Odd Fellow Adam # 273	Row 7 # 5	7/7/1909	Scotland
Schroeder, Charles	Odd Fellow San Lorenzo # 147	Row 7 # 6	7/12/1908	Germany
Johnston, Rix A.	Odd Fellow Apollo # 123	Row 7 # 7	2/12/1938	Kentucky
Peabody, Francis W.	Odd Fellow Escondido # 344	Row 7 # 8	12/1/1907	Canada
Webb, Joshua	Odd Fellow Mokelume # 44	Row 7 # 9	4/6/1907	None Listed
Volk, Adam	Odd Fellow Mariposa # 39	Row 7 # 10	8/9/1906	Germany
Cook, Ebenezer	Odd Fellow Charity # 6	Row 7 # 11	1/6/1899	New York
Murry, B. P.G.	Odd Fellow Sacramento # 2	Row 7 # 12	3/18/1899	Missouri
Clark, Jas T. P.G.	None Listed	Row 7 # 13	10/22/1897	Kentucky
Bauman, Chas	Odd Fellow Franklin # 74	Row 7 # 14	11/7/1897	Germany

Main Section

Name	Lodge	Site	Date of Death	Birthplace
Willaims, Louis	Odd Fellow Marion # 101	Row 7 # 15	11/1/1897	Prussia
Dunker, Ernest P.G.	Odd Fellow Germania # 116	Row 7 # 16	11/4/1901	Germany
Desumber, John	Odd Fellow Indian Val # 310	Row 7 # 17	7/20/1905	Prussia
Jensen, Erna	Wife	Row 7 # 18	10/8/1905	France
Jensen, Mathew P.G.	Odd Fellow Donner # 162	Row 7 # 19	6/20/1906	Prussia
Smith, William F.	None Listed	Row 8 # 1	12/10/1938	None Listed
Hake, Herman	Odd Fellow Valcano # 25	Row 8 # 2	1/14/1910	Germany
Horton, Henru P.G.	Odd Fellow Bay View # 109	Row 8 # 3	6/5/1909	England
Laramie, Charles Frank	Odd Fellow Los Angles # 35	Row 8 # 4	4/28/1909	Canada
Baker, Issac	Odd Fellow Escondido # 344	Row 8 # 5	10/17/1905	West Virginia
Brown, Andrew F.	Odd Fellows Phoenix # 239	Row 8 # 6	2/12/1908	England
Eymat, Gustau	Odd Fellow Franco American # 207	Row 8 # 7	11/24/1907	France
Hurd, Tamma	Odd Fellow Bay View # 109	Row 8 # 8	5/10/1907	New York
Baettge, John P.	Odd Fellow Germania # 116	Row 8 # 9	10/12/1906	Germany
Wood, Thomas J. P.G.	Odd Fellow Riverside # 282	Row 8 # 10	5/11/1901	South Carolina
Warnicke, Mrs. E.	Wife	Row 8 # 11	2/15/1901	Ireland
Warnicke, E.	Odd Fellow Myrtle # 275	Row 8 # 12	6/20/1910	Germany
Tufts, Matilda R.	Wife	Row 8 # 13	1/14/1912	Tennessee
Quayle, William	Odd Fellow Camptonville #307	Row 8 # 14	12/6/1901	Isle of Man
Tuffs, Oscar H.	Odd Fellow San Juan # 67	Row 8 # 15	3/2/1902	Massachusetts
Silva, Joseph	Odd Fellow Plumas # 88	Row 8 # 16	2/2/1902	Portugal
Hendrick, William P.G.	Odd Fellow Pacheco # 117	Row 8 # 17	4/21/1905	Rhode Island
Anderson, Frederick	Odd Fellow Morse # 237	Row 8 # 18	10/23/1905	Denmark
Unknown		Row 8 # 19		
Faleger, J. A.	None Listed	Row 9 # 1	1923	Non Listed
Lueders, Gustav P.G.	Odd Fellow Germania # 116	Row 9 # 2	5/4/1906	Germany
Price, Mary E.	Odd Fellow El Dorado # 8 (Wife)	Row 9 # 3	12/21/1908	Illinois
Page, T. H. P.G.	Odd Fellow Covenant # 73	Row 9 # 4	7/1/1908	Pennsylvania
Bansch, August	Odd Fellow Herman # 145	Row 9 # 5	2/16/1908	Germany
Jenney, Asa B.	Odd Fellow American # 385	Row 9 # 6	10/28/1907	New Hampshire
Roberts, William P.G.	Odd Fellow Auburn # 7	Row 9 # 7	6/10/1907	Kentucky
Singletary, Riley	Odd Fellow North Butte # 267	Row 9 # 8	11/15/1906	Ohio
De Kruze, Rudolph	Odd Fellow Placer # 38	Row 9 # 9	1/25/1903	Germany
Dillian, Frances M.	Odd Fellow Ione # 51	Row 9 # 10	3/31/1902	Missouri
Hoffman, Adam	Odd Fellow Indian Valley # 136	Row 9 # 11	12/20/1901	Germany
Raffal, Allen	Odd Fellow Greenville # 252	Row 9 # 12	8/24/1897	Virginia
Vincent, Carlos	Odd Fellow Mokelumne # 44	Row 9 # 13	12/2/1902	Canada
Watson, James	Odd Fellow Welcome # 209	Row 9 # 14	4/2/1903	Illinois
Unknown		Row 9 # 15		
Zaiss, George P.G.	Odd Fellow Mineral # 106	Row 9 # 16	11/12/1905	Germany
Blackwood, Guy K.	None Listed	Row 10 # 1	4/13/1923	None Listed
Dickinson, James P.G.	Odd Fellow Cosmopolitan # 106	Row 10 # 2	9/8/1910	England
Edwards, Samuel P.G.	Odd Fellow Rio Vista # 180	Row 10 # 3	4/25/1909	England
Laine, S. A. P.G.	Odd Fellow Telegraph # 79	Row 10 # 4	3/9/1909	Maine
Unknown		Row 10 # 5		
Jarvis, Thomas P.G.	Odd Fellow Porter # 272	Row 10 # 6	6/5/1908	England
Langdon, Chauncey P.G.	Odd Fellow Onward # 380	Row 10 # 7	12/28/1907	Vermont
Christianson	Odd Fellow Camptonville # 307	Row 10 # 8	8/12/1907	Denmark
Fleming, Mathew	Odd Fellow Jackson # 86	Row 10 # 9	12/1/1906	England
Aitkens, George K.	Odd Fellow Brooklyn # 46	Row 10 # 10	1/21/1897	Vermont
Mason, Margaret	Wife	Row 10 # 11	11/23/1902	Ireland
Mason, William Henry	Odd Fellow Charity # 6	Row 10 # 12	3/3/1905	Delaware
Carlson Jr., John	Odd Fellow Jefferson # 98	Row 10 # 13	7/10/1912	None Listed
Unknown		Row 10 # 14		

Main Section   page 4

Name	Lodge	Site	Date of Death	Birthplace
Unknown		Row 10 # 15		
Schierhold, Herman F.	Odd Fellow Concordia # 122	Row 10 # 16	10/4/1905	Germany
Garrity, Andrew	Odd Fellow Magnolia $ 20	Row 10 # 17	3/29/1903	Ireland
Unknown		Row 10 # 18		

Lower Section

Name	Lodge	Site	Date of Death	Birthplace
Wilson, Henry	Odd Fellow Wildey # 149	# 1	1/9/1897	Sweden
Guinand, B.	Odd Fellow Santa Barbara # 56	# 2	3/16/1899	Switzerland
Knight, D. P.G.	Odd Fellow Mariposa # 38	# 3	10/28/1896	Main
Patch, P. C. P.G.	Odd Fellow Greenville # 252	# 4	3/14/1896	Pennsylvania
Fredell, Henry P.G.	Odd Fellow Harmont # 13	# 5	1/18/1896	Germany
Small, John H. P.G.	Odd Fellow Charity # 6	# 6	11/18/1896	Main
Keith, Mrs. L. C.	Rebekah Azalea # 117 (Wife)	# 7	1/19/1897	Germany
Keith, L. C.	Odd Fellow Granite # 62	# 8	10/18/1895	New York
Herrick, E. D. P.G.	Odd Fellow Oustamah # 16	# 9	9/28/1895	Vermont
Meyer, Conrad	Odd Fellow Campo Seco # 10	# 10	7/16/1897	France
Rule, John	Odd Fellow San Jaun # 67	# 11	4/23/1897	Pennsylvania
Klein, George P.G.	Odd Fellow Garden City # 1421	# 12	9/17/1897	Germany
Giuliand, Tognini	Odd Fellow Laguna # 224	# 13	7/13/1897	Switzerland

3 Small Sections Not Included in Main Section Close to Phillip's Way

Name	Lodge	Site	Date of Death	Birthplace
Patterson, Jerril T.	None Listed (?? Orange Grove Rebekah # 84)	# 1	1/18/1944	Idaho
Patterson, Samuel W.	None Listed (maybe Oroville # 59)	# 2	2/8/1928	Alabama
Patterson, Susan A.	None Listed (?? Orange Grove Rebekah # 84)	# 3	9/6/1952	North Carolina
Ruby, Mark L.	None Listed (maybe Oroville # 59)	# 4	3/11/1930	Oklahoma
Cauecchia, Ann M.	None Listed (?? Orange Grove Rebekah # 84)	# 5	1972	Texas
Vaughn, John B.	None Listed (maybe Oroville # 59)	# 6	2/18/1979	None Listed
Vaughn, James W.	None Listed (maybe Oroville # 59)	# 7	5/19/1966	None Listed
Vaughn, Aleata	None Listed (?? Orange Grove Rebekah # 84)	# 7	3/3/1952	None Listed
Vaughn, Roberta J.	None Listed (?? Orange Grove Rebekah # 84)	# 8	2/2/1955	None Listed
Vaughn, William Ames	None Listed (maybe Oroville # 59)	# 8	1/2/1925 -1/4/1999	None Listed
Edwards, Georgia Ely	None Listed (?? Orange Grove Rebekah # 84)	# 9	11/22/1970	None Listed
Keith, Frank M.	None Listed (maybe Oroville # 59)	# 10	5/3/1956	None Listed
Keith, Mary L.	None Listed (?? Orange Grove Rebekah # 84)	# 11	3/12/1939	None Listed
Landers, Gertrude	None Listed (?? Orange Grove Rebekah # 84)	# 12	12/3/1925	None Listed
Cooksey, Pearl N.	None Listed (?? Orange Grove Rebekah # 84)	# 13	12/13/1959	None Listed
Day, Garly L.	None Listed (maybe Oroville # 59)	# 14	12/19/1941	None Listed
Taylor, Kiney J.	None Listed (maybe Oroville # 59)	# 15	1964	None Listed
Taylor, Elmer O.	None Listed (maybe Oroville # 59)	# 16	5/16/1961	None Listed
Inman, Dewell G.	None Listed (maybe Oroville # 59)	# 17	12/25/1965	None Listed
German, James William	None Listed (maybe Oroville # 59)	# 18	1964	None Listed
Unknown		# 19		

The maps and name lists were drawn and complied by Oroville Eagle Scout, Morgan Price October 1986

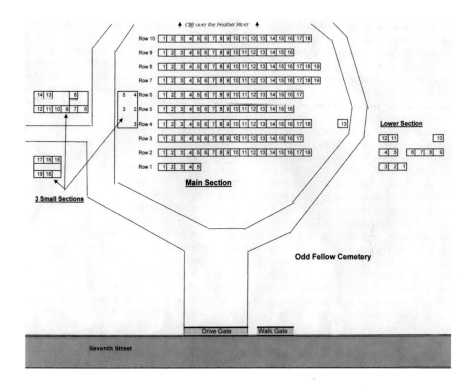

Cliff over the Feather River

Row 10 | 1 2 3 4 5 6 7 8 9 10 11 12 13 14 15 16 17 18
Row 9 | 1 2 3 4 5 6 7 8 9 10 11 12 13 14 15 16
Row 8 | 1 2 3 4 5 6 7 8 9 10 11 12 13 14 15 16 17 18 19
Row 7 | 1 2 3 4 5 6 7 8 9 10 11 12 13 14 15 16 17 18 19
Row 6 | 1 2 3 4 5 6 7 8 9 10 11 12 13 14 15 16 17
Row 5 | 1 2 3 4 5 6 7 8 9 10 11 12 13 14 15 16
Row 4 | 1 2 3 4 5 6 7 8 9 10 11 12 13 14 15 16 17 18
Row 3 | 1 2 3 4 5 6 7 8 9 10 11 12 13 14 15 16 17
Row 2 | 1 2 3 4 5 6 7 8 9 10 11 12 13 14 15 16 17 18
Row 1 | 1 2 3 4 5

Main Section

Lower Section

14 13   8
12 11 10 9 7 6

5 4
3 2
3

13

12 11   10
4 5   6 7 8 9
3 2 1

17 16 15
19 18

3 Small Sections

Odd Fellow Cemetery

Drive Gate   Walk Gate

Seventh Street

INDEX